ATLAS OF CONFLICTS

WORLD
WAR I

Stewart Ross

WORLD ALMANAC® LIBRARY

Please visit our web site at: www.worldalmanaclibrary.com
For a free color catalog describing World Almanac® Library's list of high-quality books
and multimedia programs, call 1-800-848-2928 (USA) or 1-800-387-3178 (Canada).
World Almanac® Library's fax: (414) 332-3567.

Library of Congress Cataloging-in-Publication Data

Ross, Stewart.
    World War I / by Stewart Ross.
        p. cm. — (Atlas of conflicts)
    Includes bibliographical references and index.
    ISBN 0-8368-5668-6 (lib. bdg.)
    ISBN 0-8368-5675-9 (softcover)
    1. World War, 1914-1918—Juvenile literature. 2. World War, 1914-1918—Maps
for children. I. Title: World War One. II. Title: World War 1. III. Title. IV. Series.
D521.R625   2004
940.3—dc22   2004045158

This North American edition first published in 2005 by
World Almanac® Library
330 West Olive Street, Suite 100
Milwaukee, WI 53212 USA

This U.S. edition copyright © 2005 by World Almanac® Library.
Original edition copyright © 2004 by Arcturus Publishing Limited.
Additional end matter copyright © 2005 by World Almanac® Library.

Produced by Arcturus Publishing Limited.
Series concept: Alex Woolf
Editor: Philip de Ste. Croix
Designer: Simon Burrough
Cartography: The Map Studio
Consultant: Paul Cornish, Imperial War Museum, London
Picture researcher: Thomas Mitchell

World Almanac® Library editor: Gini Holland
World Almanac® Library design: Steve Schraenkler
World Almanac® Library production: Jessica Morris

All the photographs in this book were supplied by Getty Images and are reproduced here with
their permission.

Printed in Italy

1 2 3 4 5 6 7 8 9 08 07 06 05 04

CONTENTS

CHAPTER 1
THE EUROPEAN WAR

Wilhelm II, emperor of Germany, 1888–1918, proved unequal to the task of governing his inherited empire.

Below: Irregular Macedonian fighters guard a highway leading to Salonika during the First Balkan War, 1912.

World War I, fought between 1914 and 1918, was a huge conflict that involved most of the world's major powers. Two grand alliances confronted one another: Britain, France, Russia, Italy, the United States, and others on one side (the Allies), and Germany, Austria-Hungary, Turkey, and Bulgaria (the Central Powers) on the other. The war was fought on land, at sea, and, for the first time, in the air. Advances in technology had produced powerful and deadly new weapons that changed the nature of warfare forever.

The war began in Europe. In 1871, the large, industrially developed German Empire had replaced France as the continent's major power. Needing support, France had reached an agreement ("*entente*") in 1904 with its old enemy Britain, which was also anxious about German ambitions. For many years, Britain had enjoyed good relations with most of the states that made up Germany. The British royal family was of German descent and was related to Germany's Emperor. By the 1900s, however, this traditional Anglo-German friendship was breaking down. Britain feared that its enormous colonial empire, covering one-quarter of the world's surface, was threatened by German ambitions in Africa and elsewhere. Secondly, there was serious industrial and commercial competition between the two empires. Thirdly, Britain saw the construction of a large German Navy as a direct threat to Britain's worldwide naval supremacy. By 1910, Britain and Germany were in an arms race as they tried to outdo one another in building warships.

THE BALKAN QUESTION   For centuries, the Balkan peninsula in southeast Europe had been part of the Turkish Ottoman Empire. In the nineteenth century, Turkish power declined and the Balkans broke into small, independent countries. The most politically influential were Greece, Romania, Bulgaria, Bosnia, and, especially, Serbia. In 1912–13, the intense rivalry between the Balkan countries flared into two wars.

The neighboring Russian and Austro-Hungarian Empires competed with each other for influence among the Balkan states. In 1908, for example, the Russians were furious when the Austro-Hungarians annexed Bosnia and Herzegovina. Their chief bone of

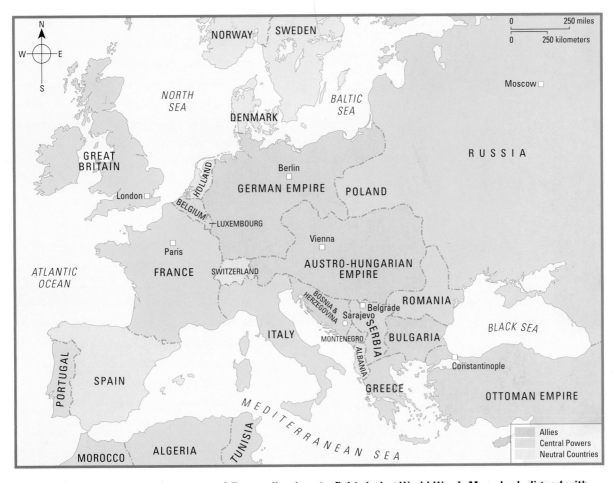

A continent divided—how the states of Europe lined up to fight during World War I. Many had aligned with one side or another long before the fighting broke out in August 1914.

contention was Serbia, which was allied with Russia and distrusted by Austria-Hungary. By 1914, these dangerous international rivalries of Europe were backed up by a series of military alliances and agreements. On the Allies' side were the countries of the Triple Entente (France, Britain, and Russia). Ranged against them were the Central Powers of Germany and Austria-Hungary, linked by a Dual Alliance and cautiously supported by Italy (which made it the Triple Alliance).

MANPOWER OF THE MAIN EUROPEAN RIVALS

Allies		**Population**	**Armed forces at outbreak of war**
Triple Entente:	Russia	167 million	5 million
	France*	39.6 million	3.78 million
	Britain*	46.4 million	733,500
Central Powers			
Dual Alliance:	Germany	67 million	4.5 million
	Austria-Hungary	49.9 million	3.35 million
Serbia (with Allies, 1914)		5 million	460,000
Italy (with Allies, from 1915)		35 million	875,000
Turkey (with Central Powers, 1914)		21.3 million	300,000?

* France and Britain could also draw on the considerable manpower of their overseas colonies.

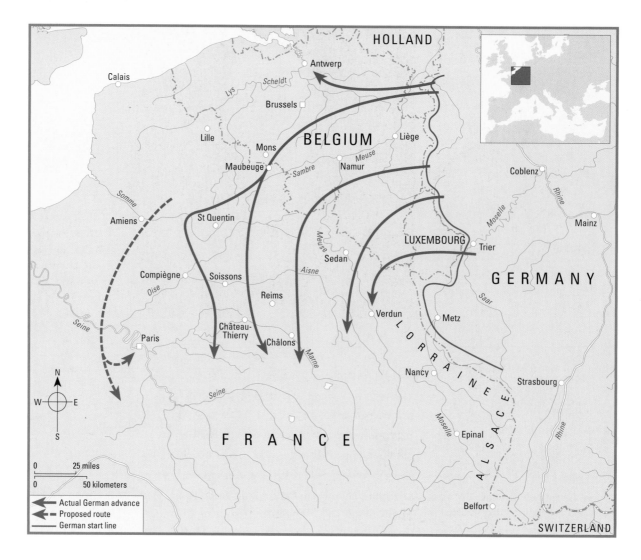

The German Schlieffen Plan envisaged a swift knockout blow in the west by driving through neutral Belgium and then surrounding Paris.

Although these alliances were in theory defensive, the colonial factor meant that a small conflict might well spread over the entire continent—and beyond.

WAR PLANS The outbreak of war in 1914 was not unexpected, and each side had made careful plans in advance. France, for instance, had long planned to attack east into Alsace and Lorraine, provinces Germany had seized in 1870–71. Predicting such a move, in 1905 German Chief of Staff General Count Alfred von Schlieffen had planned a swift attack on northern France through neutral Holland and Belgium. He believed this would quickly knock France out of the war and enable Germany to turn on Russia.

The Schlieffen Plan was altered, and weakened, by his successor, General Helmuth von Moltke. Von Moltke reduced the force attacking from the north and bypassed Holland. Nevertheless, Germany's assault on Belgium brought Britain into the war because Britain had guaranteed Belgium's neutrality.

In this tense atmosphere of the early twentieth century, the European powers were terrified of being caught unawares. If one country increased the size of its armed forces, as Germany did in 1912, its rivals immediately did the same: Russia responded to Germany's 170,000 increase by swelling its army by half a million. This in turn frightened Germany into further increases, so quickening the arms race. To meet these military requirements, all the major countries except Britain required young men to participate in military service.

THE ARMS RACE

Sir Edward Grey, Britain's foreign secretary at the outbreak of war, outlined the process of the arms race: *"One nation increases its army and makes strategic railways towards the frontiers of neighboring countries. The second nation makes counter-strategic railways and increases its army in reply. The first nation says this is very unreasonable, because its own military preparations were only precautions, and points out . . . that the first nation began the competition; and so it goes on, till the whole Continent is an armed camp covered by strategic railways."*

—From *Twenty-five Years,*
1892–1916,
Viscount E. Grey

Left: Helmuth von Moltke, the German commander whose failure to execute the Schlieffen Plan led to his dismissal in 1914.

Britain's iron shield: headed by the battleship HMS *Neptune*, the Royal Navy displays its power at the 1911 Spithead Fleet Review.

The gigantic Russian army had the reputation of being a "steamroller"—slow to get going but unstoppable once on the move. Furthermore, it was growing larger by the day, and Russia itself was developing mass-produced weapons. The German command feared that the longer war was delayed, the less chance they had of winning. Consequently, when German ally Austria-Hungary threatened war with Serbia in July 1914, the German Emperor Wilhelm II gave his full backing: If war was to come, his generals argued, then the sooner the better.

INTO BATTLE The outbreak of war was sparked by the assassination of Archduke Franz Ferdinand, heir to the throne of Austria-Hungary, on June 28, 1914. The Austro-Hungarians blamed Serbian terrorists for the outrage and declared war on Serbia on July 28, 1914. This started a domino effect. When Russia prepared to help Serbia, Germany declared war on it (August 1). France, Russia's ally, mobilized its troops, so Germany declared war on it, too. This launched the Schlieffen Plan, which brought Britain into the spreading conflict (August 4, 1914). The Schlieffen

Plan very nearly succeeded. The Germans drove back the French in the east and moved through Belgium to within 30 miles (50 km) of Paris by late August. France, with British help, halted the offensive on the River Marne, ending German hopes of a swift victory.

The Battle of the Marne, officially September 5–9, 1914, was the first in which aircraft played a vital role. The Schlieffen Plan had called for the German armies to encircle Paris from the west. However, finding his enemy in disarray, the commander of the German First Army, General Alexander von Kluck, advanced across the Marne to the east of the capital. This move was spotted by Allied aircraft. The French commander, Marshal Joseph Joffre, responded with an attack on Kluck's unguarded right flank—and the Germans were forced to withdraw.

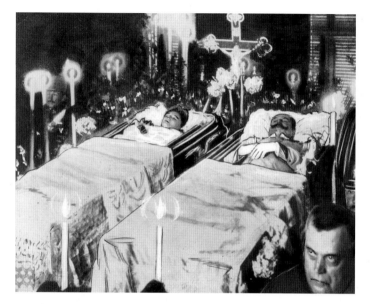

Left: Two deaths that led to millions more. The bodies of the Austrian Archduke Franz Ferdinand and his wife Sophie lie in state.

Below: The Battle of the Marne, September 1914. By halting the German advance, the Allies ensured a long and bitter conflict.

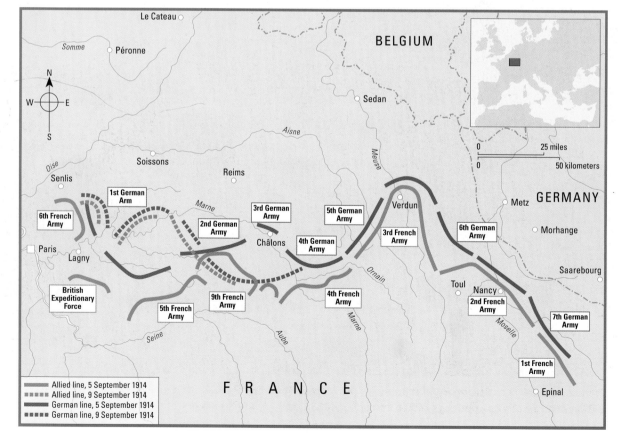

The battle was one of the most decisive of modern history. The failure of the Schlieffen Plan forced Germany to fight on two fronts, in the west against Britain and France, and in the east against Russia. In the end, this proved more than Germany could stand. Moreover, the battle virtually ended the war of movement in Western Europe. Unable to out-maneuver each other, the two sides swiftly burrowed in for years of drawn-out, costly trench warfare (*see pages 10-11*) in which neither side gained much ground.

TRENCH WARFARE The classic strategy of armies facing one another is to seek to outflank (get around behind) their enemy. This is precisely what the

TIMETABLE OF THE BATTLE OF THE MARNE, 1914

Aug. 14–25	Germans advance on all fronts towards Paris.
Aug. 31	Germans within 30 miles (50 km) of Paris.
Sept. 4	General Kluck moves southeast of Paris, crossing River Marne, and his forces are seen by Allied spotter planes.
Sept. 5	French forces meet advancing German 1st Army. British join the counter offensive.
Sept. 6	French and British counterattack on Kluck's right flank.
Sept. 6–8	Fierce fighting all along the line.
Sept. 9	Kluck orders his army to withdraw. German commander in chief General von Moltke orders withdrawal to the River Aisne, north of Paris.

French soldiers in action during the Battle of the Marne, September 1914. At this early stage of the war, soldiers were not equipped with either camouflaged uniforms or steel helmets.

Below: Temporary shelters that became home—German soldiers in hastily constructed trenches, 1914.

TROUBLE WITH WATER

One of the great problems of trench warfare, as Captain J. I. Cohen wrote from Ypres in 1915, was drainage:

"This horrible country is made of mud, water and dead Germans. Whenever water is left in a trench it drags the earth down on either side and forms a fearfully sticky viscous matter that lets you sink gently down and grips you like a vice when you're there. . . . Cover is got by building . . . dug-outs, behind the trench. Two walls of sandbags with a sheet of corrugated iron on top and an oil-sheet under it to make the whole waterproof."

—Quoted in *The Imperial War Museum Book of the First World War,* edited by Malcolm Brown

Allies (French and British) and the Germans tried to do after the Battle of the Marne. As one side moved, however, so the other side moved with them. This stretched the front line so that it eventually ran from the Belgian coast to the Swiss border.

Improved military technology—in particular, machine guns, barbed wire, and heavy artillery—made a frontal attack almost impossible. To protect themselves, troops on either side dug lines of trenches, usually three deep. These filthy, dangerous holes became the hallmark of the war, both on the Western Front and elsewhere.

World War I was the first to be fought between large industrialized nations. Power depended as much upon industrial output—ships, artillery, rifles, and so forth—as on human muscle. Pinned down by barbed wire, and at the mercy of streams of quick-fire bullets and bombardment by high-explosive shells, the individual soldier became just a statistic: categorized as able-bodied, wounded, or dead. The war they fought had little to do with glory or valor; it was about "attrition," grinding the enemy down until they (or you) could take no more.

The trench line from Switzerland to the English Channel was complete by the beginning of winter. At the time, it was not seen as permanent. On October 30, 1914, for example, the Germans began a series of attacks on a salient (bulge) in the Allied line around

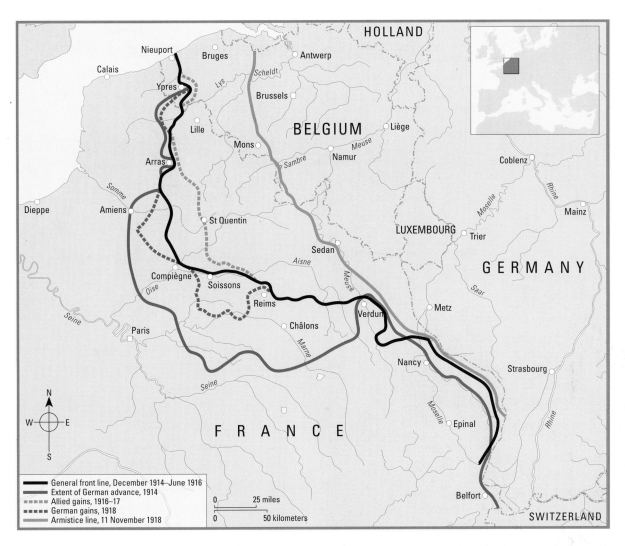

Above: The Western Front, 1914–18. The dominance of defensive technology meant that the line moved little in over four years of fighting.

Map legend:
- General front line, December 1914–June 1916
- Extent of German advance, 1914
- Allied gains, 1916–17
- German gains, 1918
- Armistice line, 11 November 1918

0 — 25 miles
0 — 50 kilometers

the town of Ypres in Belgium. The fighting lasted until November 24. Although very little ground was gained, the casualties were shocking: 58,200 British, some 50,000 French, and 134,300 Germans. The full horror of mechanized (trench) warfare began to show its face.

THE EASTERN FRONT, 1914–15

The Russian Empire entered the war with enthusiasm. Loyalty to the all-powerful Russian emperor, Nicholas II, swelled, and his massive armies assembled faster than anticipated. By mid-August 1914, two Russian armies, commanded by Generals Pavel Rennenkampf and Alexander Samsonov, were advancing into Prussia, northeastern Germany. However, although moving less

French soldiers operate a captured German machine gun. Weapons like this took a terrible toll of human life in the war of attrition on the Western Front.

Above: Splendid-looking but ineffective—as with all cavalry, these Russian Cossacks were easy targets for machine gun and artillery fire.

Right: The Eastern Front along which the mighty Russian Empire battled against the empires of Germany and Austria-Hungary.

slowly than expected, they also proved easier to halt.

The Russian commanders did not get along, which made communication between their two armies poor at best. Furthermore, the German commanders, Generals Paul von Hindenburg and Erich Ludendorff, managed to pick up uncoded Russian radio signals. These gave invaluable information about Russian troop numbers and movements to Germany.

In late August, the Germans split the Russian armies and

CASUALTIES ON THE EASTERN FRONT, 1914

	Killed or wounded	Taken prisoner
Russian	617,000	182,000
German	115,000	–
Austro-Hungarian	400,000	100,000

These appalling statistics reveal that in just five months of fighting well over a million soldiers had been lost and over one-quarter of a million taken prisoner. The Russians alone had lost almost 800,000 (including those killed, wounded, and captured).

crushed Samsonov's isolated force around the town of Tannnenberg in East Prussia. After the battle (August 26–30) the disgraced Russian commander committed suicide. The Germans then turned on Rennenkampf, outmaneuvered him, and defeated him at the Battle of Masurian Lakes (September 9–14). By autumn of 1914, the Russians were once more back behind their own frontiers.

Further south, in Galicia, the Russians faced the armies of the Austro-Hungarian Empire. Ruled since the thirteenth century by the Hapsburg family, the Austro-Hungarian Empire was one of the oldest in Europe. Its territory stretched from Bohemia (modern-day Czech Republic) to Bosnia in the Balkans.

The idea behind this European empire of many peoples and cultures was somewhat out of date. Held together by a vast bureaucracy and loyalty to Emperor Franz Joseph I, its multicultual force was less well-suited to industrial war than Germany's. In Galicia, after initial setbacks, the Russians pushed the multi-national Austro-Hungarian forces back and advanced along a wide front until halted by the rugged Carpathian Mountains.

By Christmas 1914, the situation on much of the Eastern Front was similar to the trench warfare in the West, although less rigid. Millions of men, sheltered within frozen trenches, faced each other across barely 109 yards (100 meters) of barren "no-man's-land."

Too young to die? Russian prisoners of war after the decisive Battle of the Masurian Lakes, September 1914, included this very young soldier.

THE BALKANS Given the region's troubled history (the mixture of peoples of different ethnic backgrounds and religious beliefs had led to many conflicts in the past), it is little surprise that the fighting in the Balkans was as ferocious and costly as anywhere. It began in 1914 with a massive Austro-Hungarian attack on Serbia. Fighting to defend their native land, the Serbs proved fierce fighters. Out of a population of some five million, they raised an army of half a million and even drew on the services of women. The invaders were repeatedly driven back with heavy losses.

In 1915, the tide turned. Bulgaria joined the war on the side of the Central Powers and Germany sent 300,000 troops to assist its ally. Utterly overwhelmed, the Serbs fought on to the end of year, and some escaped to join Allied forces elsewhere. Nevertheless, by 1916, Serbia was out of the war and Austria-Hungary's power now reached to the frontiers of Greece and Albania.

Romania, wooed by both sides, eventually joined the war on the side of the Allies in August 1916. It proved a costly mistake. Russia was by this time exhausted, leaving the 500,000-strong Romanian army exposed to an attack by a combined force of Austro-Hungarians, Bulgarians, Turks, and Germans. By the

KNOWING THE TERRAIN

A British journalist describes how the Serbian commander General Mishitch used his local knowledge to defeat the Austro-Hungarian attack of December 1914:

"*He suddenly advanced in a general attack, on the morning of December 3rd, 1914, and completely surprised the Austro-Hungarians. He caught them leisurely moving along the valley paths. Capturing the overlooking hills, the Serbs shot the hostile columns down, while the Austro-Hungarians were still wondering where they should place their artillery. Naturally, the Serbs knew every rise and fall of the ground, for Mishitch himself had been born and bred [there].*"

—Quoted in *The Great War*, edited by H.W. Wilson and J. A. Hammerton

end of the year, Bucharest, the capital city of Romania, had fallen. Four hundred thousand men and three-quarters of the country's territory were lost.

Another area of fighting in the Balkans was at Salonika, a port in neutral Greece. Here, in an attempt

British soldiers in a cheerful mood after landing at Salonika in Greece on their way to reinforce their hard-pressed Serbian allies to the north.

to assist Serbia in 1915, the Allies landed a force of British and French troops that moved north toward Serbia. It came too late to help the Serbs, however, and was too small to do much on its own. Relatively secure behind their barbed wire, the Allied troops made no notable advance until September 1918. By then, the war was almost over. Extraordinarily, the maintenance of the Salonika Front cost almost 500,000 casualties—18,000 from the war and the rest from disease.

Left: Surprising many, Serbia held out against the numerically superior Austro-Hungarians and fell to the Central Powers only when German troops joined the invasion in 1915.

A Serbian howitzer prepares to fire on the invading Austrians, 1915. With no direct link to the sea, Serbia could not easily receive Allied munitions.

CHAPTER 2
THE FIGHTING SPREADS

Above: Unsuccessfully seeking the Gallipoli break-out: an Allied heavy field gun in action at Helles Bay on the tip of the Gallipoli peninsula, 1915.

The Turkish Ottoman Empire, a friend of Germany before the war, entered the conflict on the side of the Central Powers in November 1914. This had little immediate impact on the conflict, other than threatening British-held Egypt and forcing Russia to open yet another front to the east of the Black Sea. The following year, however, Turkey was involved in a major campaign that, had it succeeded, might have altered the whole course of the war.

In February and March 1915, British and French warships tried to force their way through the Dardanelles, the narrow neck of water that links the Mediterranean to the Black Sea. The aim, strongly backed by Britain's Winston Churchill, then the First Lord of the Admiralty, was to seize Constantinople (modern-day Istanbul) and open a sea route to Russia. Had this been achieved, there was a possibility that the Allies would be able to threaten the Central Powers from Russia's borders on the east.

LANDING AT GALLIPOLI

The Allies' naval operation was a failure. Three ships were sunk by Turkish mines and the heavy shore guns remained intact. Undaunted, the Allies turned to a different strategy: a landing on the Gallipoli Peninsula than runs up the western side of the Dardanelles. In April, 75,000 British, French, and Anzac (Australia and New Zealand Army Corps) men went ashore at different points on the toe of the peninsula. Some met almost no resistance and, had they pressed inland, might have quickly secured a sound base.

The Allied commanders were too hesitant or simply incompetent, and the advantage was lost. The Turkish resistance, well organized by the German General Liman von Sanders, kept the Allies pinned down on the beaches. A second landing in August was also ineffective.

Left: The Gallipoli Campaign, 1915–16. Although daring and original in concept, the Allied plan failed through gross mismanagement on the ground and because of the courage of the Turkish resistance.

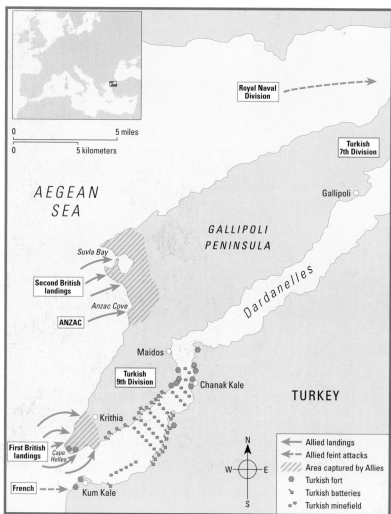

AEGEAN SEA

Royal Naval Division

Turkish 7th Division

Gallipoli

GALLIPOLI PENINSULA

Suvla Bay

Second British landings

Anzac Cove

ANZAC

Dardanelles

Maidos

Turkish 9th Division

Chanak Kale

TURKEY

Krithia

First British landings

Cape Helles

French

Kum Kale

0   5 miles
0   5 kilometers

N
W — E
S

→ Allied landings
⇠ Allied feint attacks
▨ Area captured by Allies
● Turkish fort
⚓ Turkish batteries
⁂ Turkish minefield

Going nowhere—British troops at Gallipoli try to advance beyond the beaches, August 1915. Time and again they were thrown back by the well-organized Turkish defenses.

In October the decision was made to withdraw, an operation completed by January 1916. So ended one of the major fiascos of the war, a dismal catalog of poor planning and incompetent leadership that produced some 250,000 casualties on either side.

NORTHERN ITALY Italy's agreements with Germany and Austria-Hungary did not require it to enter the war on their side in 1914. This was just as well because, at the time, its armed forces were in poor shape—there were only six hundred machine guns in the entire country, for example. Nevertheless, the temptation to join the war proved too great, and the following year (May 1915) Italy sided with the Allies in the hope of gaining territory from Austria-Hungary.

The war did not go well for the Italians. They remained short of weapons and munitions, both of which were supplied in large quantities by Britain and France. Furthermore, the Austro-Hungarians held the key strategic positions in the mountains overlooking Italian lines (*see facing map on page 19 showing Italian positions in relation to Austro-Hungarian movements*).

Fighting the enemy – and the weather. Troops of the Italian Alpine Regiment prepare for action in the snowy Alps, 1915.

The American novelist Ernest Hemingway served as a volunteer with an ambulance unit on the Italian Front. He based his novel *A Farewell to Arms* (1929) directly on his experiences. This is how he describes the scene in the first chapter of the book:

"There were mists over the river and clouds on the mountain and the trucks splashed mud on the road and the troops were muddy and wet in their capes; their rifles were wet …

At the start of the winter came permanent rain and with the rain came cholera. But it was checked and in the end only seven thousand died of it in the army."

—From *A Farewell to Arms*, Ernest Hemingway

day, and the Italian withdrawal halted only on the River Piave, about 68 miles (110 km) from the Isonzo. Around 275,000 Italians had been captured.

The Italians eventually dug in and rebuilt on the Piave. Assisted by Allied reinforcements, Italy's new commander, General Armando Diaz, launched a final offensive in October 1918 against an enemy that was by now exhausted from sustaining years of fighting on two fronts. The Allies advanced swiftly along a broad

Left: Austrian troops, armed with flame-throwers, advance along the Isonzo River, 1916.

Below: The front in northeastern Italy. The easy gains that Italy hoped for when it joined the war in 1915 were not forthcoming.

Austria-Hungary found it hard enough to manage its long front with Russia, so in the beginning it was content to resist Italian assaults. Between 1915–17, the Italians launched eleven full-scale offensives in the region, none of which managed to seize more than a few miles of ground. After the last offensive, made in the late summer of 1917, the Italian commander General Luigi Cadorna decided to build up his defenses to face an expected attack by German as well as Austro-Hungarian forces.

The Central Powers' attack of October 24–November 12, 1917, known as the Battle of Caporetto, was a total disaster for the Italian Army. German forces advanced about 14 miles (23 km) on the first

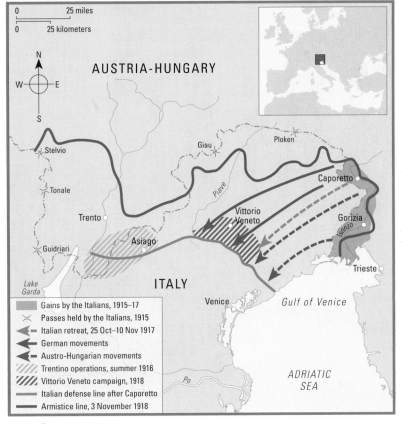

0	25 miles
0	25 kilometers

AUSTRIA-HUNGARY

Stelvio
Giau
Ploken
Caporetto
Tonale
Piave
Trento
Vittorio Veneto
Gorizia
Guidriari
Asiago
Isonzo
Trieste
Lake Garda
ITALY
Venice
Gulf of Venice
Po
ADRIATIC SEA

Gains by the Italians, 1915–17
Passes held by the Italians, 1915
Italian retreat, 25 Oct–10 Nov 1917
German movements
Austro-Hungarian movements
Trentino operations, summer 1916
Vittorio Veneto campaign, 1918
Italian defense line after Caporetto
Armistice line, 3 November 1918

British General Edmund Allenby rides into Jerusalem, Palestine, after driving the Turks from the city, December 1917.

front until Austria-Hungary signed an armistice on November 3, 1918, bringing hostilities between that country and the Allies to a close (*see also page 50*).

MIDDLE EAST The war extended into the Middle East when the fleet of the Turkish Ottoman Empire bombarded Russian Black Sea ports without warning on October 29, 1914. Declarations of war soon followed. In alliance with the Central Powers, who provided officers and munitions for the depleted Turkish Army, Turkey fought on four fronts. On only one, Gallipoli (*see pages 14-15*), did it achieve success.

In the north, the Turks launched an attack on southern Russia (the Caucasus) in an attempt to seize the region's oilfields. At the Battle of Sarikamish (December 29, 1914 to January 3, 1915) they were soundly defeated, suffering 30,000 casualties and losing much of their remaining army as prisoners of war.

SETTING UP MAJOR CONFLICT

Eager for support, British politicians made conflicting offers to their allies. They promised the Arabs independence and the Jews a national homeland in Palestine. Foreign Minister Lord Balfour's letter to Lord Rothschild, the leader of Britain's Jews, proved to be one of the seeds of the modern Arab-Israeli conflict.

"His Majesty's Government view with favour the establishment in Palestine of a national home for the Jewish people, and will use their best endeavours to facilitate the achievement of this object, it being clearly understood that nothing shall be done which may prejudice the civil and religious rights of existing non-Jewish communities in Palestine, or the rights and political status enjoyed by Jews in any other country."–November 2, 1917.

—Quoted in *Arab-Israeli Conflict and Conciliation: A Documentary History*, edited by Bernard Reich

In the eastern corner of their empire, in the region of Mesopotamia (modern-day Iraq) at the head of the Persian Gulf, the Turks faced an invasion by an Anglo-Indian army sent from British-held India. At first, the invaders made swift progress, taking the region's oil fields. The Turks regained the initiative in 1916 when they took 8,000 Anglo-Indian prisoners at Kut al Imara. By the time hostilities ended, however, the British had again moved forward, capturing Baghdad (March 1917) and advancing further up the Tigris and Euphrates rivers.

The Suez Canal in Egypt, a key route between Britain and India (then the jewel in Britain's imperial crown) was an obvious target for the Turks. Knowing this, the British built up strong defenses, resisted Turkish assaults in 1914–15, and pressed on into Sinai in 1916–17. They were assisted by a widespread revolt among the Arab peoples, eager to be rid of their Turkish overlords.

Held up for a while at Gaza, at the end of 1917 the Allies seized Jerusalem in Palestine. The large Anglo-Arab force, commanded by General

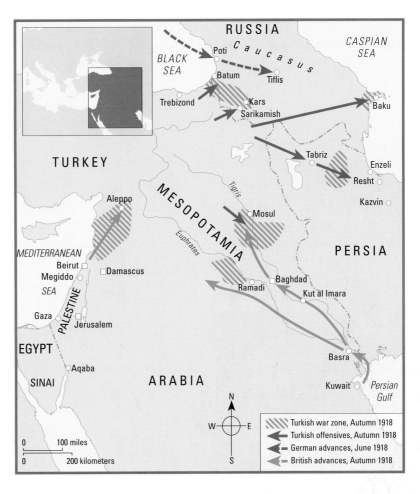

Above: Fighting in the Near and Middle East, where the Turkish Ottoman Empire fought the Russians and the British and also struggled to hold down a revolt of the Arabs.

Map labels:
RUSSIA — CASPIAN SEA — BLACK SEA — Caucasus — Poti — Batum — Tiflis — Trebizond — Kars — Sarikamish — Baku — Tabriz — Enzeli — Resht — Kazvin — TURKEY — Aleppo — Mosul — Tigris — MESOPOTAMIA — PERSIA — Euphrates — MEDITERRANEAN — Beirut — Damascus — Megiddo — SEA — Baghdad — Ramadi — Kut al Imara — PALESTINE — Gaza — Jerusalem — EGYPT — Aqaba — SINAI — ARABIA — Basra — Kuwait — Persian Gulf

0   100 miles
0   200 kilometers

Turkish war zone, Autumn 1918
Turkish offensives, Autumn 1918
German advances, June 1918
British advances, Autumn 1918

Battling for the British Empire—Indian gunners defend the British-held Suez Canal against a Turkish attack.

Edmund Allenby, then destroyed the remaining Turkish forces in the region at the Battle of Megiddo and moved forward to occupy Damascus in Syria on October 1, 1918.

AFRICA The Middle East was not the limit of the fighting. The conflict became truly global as early as 1914, when Japan, an ally of Britain, seized German colonies in the Pacific Ocean and in mainland China. There was fighting in Africa, too. Here Allied

LOSSES IN AFRICA

Cameroons

Britain	2,300 killed, wounded, and captured
France	3,900 killed, wounded, and captured
Germany	6,575 killed, wounded, and captured

South-West Africa

South Africa	1,760 killed, wounded, and captured
Germany	4,580 killed, wounded, and captured

East Africa

Allies	51,600 killed or died of disease
	8,800 wounded
	1,900 captured
Germany*	5,000 killed and wounded
	6,000 captured

* Figures are no more than estimates

Left: War East African style: A British soldier seated on an ox during the long campaign to hunt down German General Paul von Lettow-Vorbeck.

Cameroons, 1914–17. On the outbreak of war, South Africa offered to undertake the capture of German South-West Africa. This was achieved by four columns, totalling 50,000 men, over a period of ten months.

In contrast, German resistance in East Africa continued throughout the war. This was largely due to the leadership of German General Paul von Lettow-Vorbeck, a brilliant guerrilla commander. In 1914, he had a mere 2,750 men (of whom 2,500 were Africans) to hold a territory the size of France. Later this rose to 14,000 (including 11,000 Africans). Against him were ranged almost the entire South African Army and many European and local troops and assistants, totalling, at their peak, 350,000 men. This was precisely what Lettow-Vorbeck wanted—to divert as many Allied soldiers as possible

forces from Britain, France, and their colonies attacked Germany's four African colonies: Togoland (Togo), the Cameroons (Cameroon), German South-West Africa (Namibia), and German East Africa (Tanzania). They wanted to seize territory and shut down the German radio stations that were monitoring Allied shipping.

Togo fell swiftly to French and British troops in 1914. The same two countries gradually occupied the

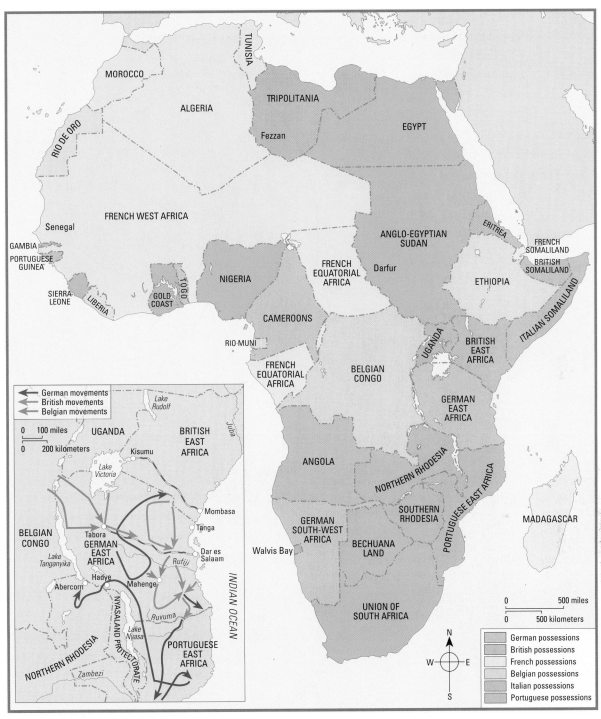

Africa during World War I. The continent was dragged into the fighting because, during the previous century, it had been carved into colonies by the imperial European powers, many of which were now fighting for or against one another. The inset shows the campaign in German East Africa.

from the battles in Europe (*see statistics box on page 22*), to help Germany achieve victory there.

After a successful but costly attack early in 1915, Lettow-Vorbeck decided to stick to hit-and-run guerrilla tactics. He used local conditions and speed of movement to great effect. A successful tactic was to build up a strong defensive position, hold it for a while in order to inflict maximum casualties on the attackers, then slip away before the final assault. Only when he heard of the Armistice (*see page 49*) did the

COMPARATIVE NAVAL STRENGTHS, 1914

Allies	Britain	France	Russia	Italy	Japan	U.S.*	Totals
New-style battleships (dreadnoughts)	22	8	0	3	2	10	45
Old-style battleships	40	14	10	7	10	23	104
Cruisers	130	28	12	21	34	34	259
Destroyers	221	81	25	33	50	50	460
Torpedo boats	109	187	72	80	0	23	471
Submarines	73	70	22	23	12	18	218

* By the time the United States entered the war in 1917, all fleets were larger.

Central Powers	Germany	Aus.-Hungary	Turkey	Totals
New-style battleships (dreadnoughts)	15	6	0	21
Old-style battleships	22	6	2	30
Cruisers	57	7	2	66
Destroyers	90	18	8	116
Torpedo boats	115	65	9	189
Submarines	31	5	0	36

The foredeck and main guns of the German battleship *Braunschweig,* pictured here at the start of the war in 1914.

undefeated Lettow-Vorbeck finally surrender on November 23, 1918.

WAR AT SEA Naval warfare had been revolutionized during the fifty years before 1914. Huge steel battleships, driven by steam turbines and armed with massive shell-firing guns in turrets, had made all other large warships obsolete. However, these remarkable vessels were vulnerable to mines (*as we saw in the Dardanelles, pages 16-17*) and torpedoes. The latter could now be delivered with great accuracy by submarines. Finally, the use of spotter aircraft and radio enabled commanders to know their enemy's precise location and movements.

Essentially, the naval war developed into one of blockades—the Allies sought to cut Germany and Austria-Hungary's overseas supplies of food and raw materials, while the Germans tried to do the same to Britain and France. In the end, it was the Allied blockade that succeeded, bringing Germany to its knees in the autumn of 1918.

Germany's chief hope of breaking the Allied blockade lay in sailing its High Seas Fleet past the British Grand Fleet into the open oceans. After some

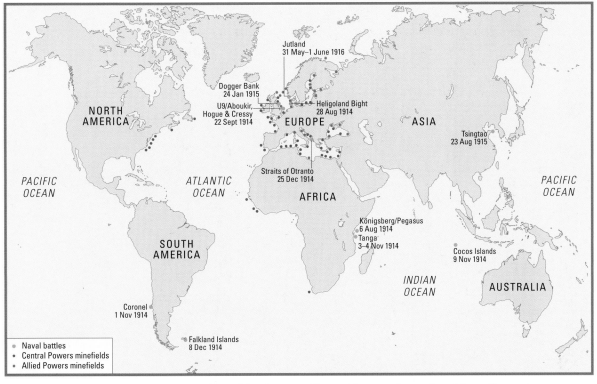

early naval encounters at Coronel and the Falkland Islands (both 1914), and in the North Sea (1914-15), Admiral Reinhard Scheer decided to attempt this full-scale break-out in May 1916. The German High Seas Fleet met the British Grand Fleet at the Battle of Jutland, the only major naval engagement of World War I. The British suffered greater losses but drove the Germans back to port, where they stayed for the rest of the war. After Jutland, the Germans relied on submarines, known as U-boats, to cut Allied supply lines. For an effective blockade, U-boats needed to attack all shipping—neutral or Allied—destined for Britain and France. This tactic infuriated the United States and helped bring it into the war on the Allied side in April 1917. By 1918, the Allies used convoys and improved antisubmarine weapons (such as the depth charge, 1916) to break the U-boat's dangerous stranglehold.

WAR IN THE AIR The wartime development of aircraft technology was dramatic, driven mainly by the need to conduct aerial observation of enemy artillery and to prevent the enemy from doing this themselves. In 1914, warplanes were slow, fairly unreliable, incapable of carrying heavy loads, and used

Above: The naval war. Apart from the major engagement between the British and German fleets at Jutland, 1916, conflicts were small scale, involving no more than a handful of vessels on either side.

A Fairey F.17 seaplane, 1917. The emergence of such aircraft enabled fleet commanders to keep track of the enemy with much greater accuracy.

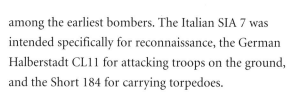

Above: A German naval Zeppelin airship taking off from its base. Although capable of flying huge distances, Zeppelins were slow and vulnerable to enemy fire.

Right: Early bombing—a British air crew prepares to drop its aircraft's lightweight bombs by hand. Inevitably, the accuracy of the bombing was poor.

largely for reconnaissance work. By 1918, they had become much more powerful and reliable and were designed with specific tasks in mind. They were also organized into a separate branch of the armed forces, such as the Royal Air Force (1918), and were seen as a vital element in any military or naval operation. Air superiority, which the Allies had achieved by 1918, was key to success on the ground. The major Allied offensive of September 1918, for example, took place under cover provided by over 450 aircraft.

One of the first specialist aircraft to appear was the fast and maneuverable fighter, designed to shoot down enemy aircraft in "dogfights." A popular example was the British Sopwith Camel. The French Breugets were among the earliest bombers. The Italian SIA 7 was intended specifically for reconnaissance, the German Halberstadt CL11 for attacking troops on the ground, and the Short 184 for carrying torpedoes.

A German speciality was the gas-filled airship, known as the Zeppelin, used for long-range bombing. Able to rise to about 22,000 feet (6,700 m), higher than any aircraft before 1916, and carry 2,205 pounds (1,000 kg) of bombs, they killed 550 civilians in raids on Britain. Once aircraft could reach the same height as a Zeppelin, however, the cumbersome "sausages" (as they were known) became easy targets.

In 1918 two aircraft appeared that pointed to the future. One was Germany's sleek and rapid Junkers D1,

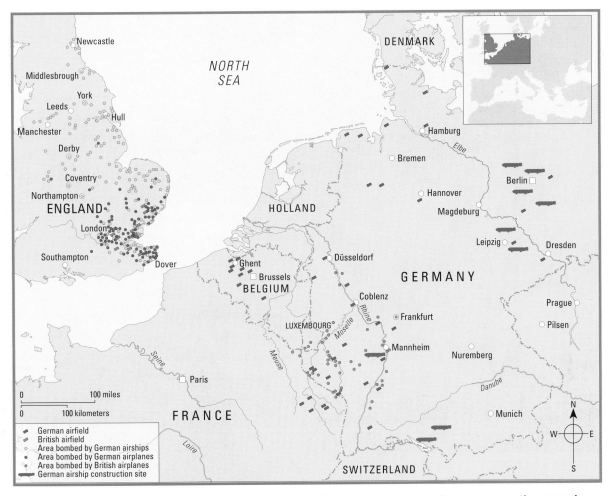

The war in the air. This map shows how the use of aircraft as bombers meant that no one on the ground, neither soldier nor civilian, was safe from attack.

the world's first all-metal warplane. The other was Britain's Handley Page V/1500, a four-engined bomber capable of carrying 4,410 pounds (2,000 kg) of bombs and staying airborne for fourteen hours. With aircraft such these, no one, neither soldier nor civilian, was safe. Thus World War I saw the emergence of the "home front"—war waged against the civil population of a country—alongside the traditional battle front.

THE GROWTH OF AIR FORCES

Number of aircraft	France	Britain*	Italy	U.S.	Russia	Germany	A-Hungary
1914	150	50	120		145	250	80
1915	390	153	240		553	800	112
1916	1,420	410	430		724	1,550	144
1917	2,335	997	660	55	579	2,270	296
1918	3,222	1,799	720	740	260	2,710	616

* Western Front only
 Note that not all of these aircraft were of military use. Of the 55 aircraft available to the United States in April 1917, for instance, 51 were obsolete.

CHAPTER 3
DEADLOCK, 1915–17

During 1915, particularly after the failure of the Allied Gallipoli expedition (*see pages 16-17*), it was generally recognized that the fight on the Western Front was now critical and that the war would be won or lost there. Here, at the direct interface between Germany, France, and Britain—where the front lines confronted one another—the fighting became more and more costly.

At the start of the year, commanders on both sides, especially the Allied one, hoped that a quick breakthrough would end the stalemate on the Western Front and bring the war to a rapid conclusion. As they found time and time again, however, seizing three lines of enemy trenches was difficult enough, but co-ordinating an advance after that proved just about impossible. In March 1915, for example, the British broke through at Neuve-Chapelle in northern France but, after advancing a mere 1.25 miles (2 km), the attack ground to a halt. The story was similar the next month, when the Germans, using poison gas for the first time, broke through at Ypres in Belgium. When the

Above: One of the millions of victims—a French soldier killed in the 1915 campaign in the Champagne region.

Below: A walk in hell: German reinforcements move up to the front line during the Champagne offensive of 1915.

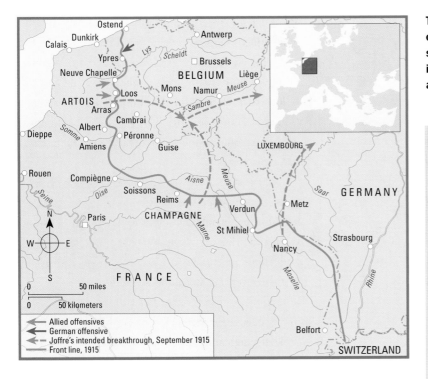

battle stopped on May 25, they had only been able to flatten the Ypres salient. For these small gains, German and Allied casualties totalled 103,000.

In the same month of May 1915, the British and French went on the offensive again, this time in the Artois region. As before, in some places the attackers managed to break through the enemy lines but they made little progress after that. September saw the launch of a massive offensive that was to smash through the German lines in Champagne and allow the French to sweep north into Belgium. After a 2,500-gun bombardment, 500,000 French troops attacked along a 15-mile (24-km) front. The same pattern emerged: some initial gains, then stagnation, and horrific casualty rates. By September 28, the French had lost 145,000 men.

As the Champagne offensive was grinding to a halt, an Anglo-French offensive started further north in the Artois region of France. The French lost 48,000 men for negligible gains, while the incompetent leadership of Sir John French, commander of the British army in France, bungled the promising British breakthrough around the village of Loos , from September 25 to November 4.

THE BATTLE AT VERDUN Unknown to each other, both sides planned even bigger offensives for 1916. They hoped for a breakthrough, of course, but there was a growing recognition that this might not be possible. In its place came the concept of attrition (*see pages 10–11*)—a war that would be won only when the enemy was either too depleted or too exhausted to fight on.

IN THE FRONT LINES

Although it is a novel, *All Quiet on the Western Front* by the German soldier Erich Remarque is widely recognized as one of the finest accounts of life on the Western Front. This is his description of bombardment:

"An uncertain red glow spreads along the skyline from one end to the other. It is in perpetual movement, punctuated with bursts of flame from the nozzles of the batteries … French rockets go up, which unfold a silk parachute to the air and drift slowly down. They light up everything as bright as day … 'Bombardment,' says Kat. The thunder of the guns swells to a single heavy roar and then breaks up again into separate explosions. The dry bursts of the machine guns rattle. Above us, the air teems with invisible swift movement, with howls, pipings, and hisses …"

—From *All Quiet On the Western Front*, Erich Remarque

While the Allies planned a summer offensive near the Somme River, at the junction of the French and British armies, the German commander General Erich von Falkenhayn hoped to break France's spirit by continual assault on a narrow front that was difficult to defend. His target was

Above: French troops defending their line at Verdun go over the top of their trenches in a counteroffensive against the encircling Germans in 1916.

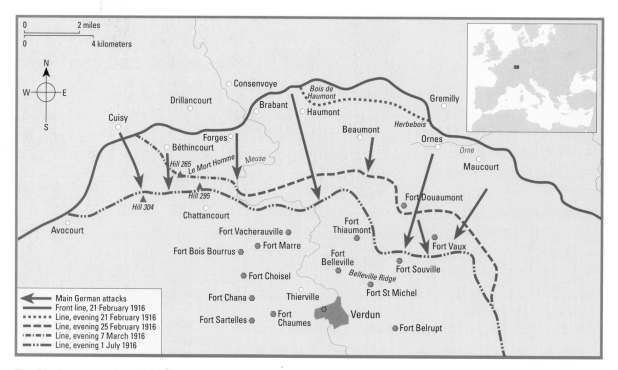

The Verdun campaign of 1916. Although the Germans made some significant gains, they failed to break through or crush the spirit of the French Army.

VERDUN IN PERSPECTIVE

French and German losses in just this one battle of Verdun in 1916 exceeded those of all major combatant nations during fighting in the previous year.

Losses in 1915

	French	British	German	Total
Neuve-Chapelle	-	13,000	7,000	20,000
Ypres	10,000	59,000	35,000	104,000
Artois	102,000	28,000	49,000	179,000
Champagne	143,000		85,000	228,000
Artois-Loos	48,000	61,000	56,000	165,000
	303,000	**161,000**	**232,000**	**696,000**

Losses in the Battle of Verdun, 1916

French	378,000
German	337,000
	715,000

Verdun, a city that (because of its historical importance as a fortress since Roman times) he knew the French would defend to the last man. Here, he undertook to "bleed" the French army to death. The German attack on Verdun began on February 21, 1916. One million men launched themselves on a network of forts that had been left under-manned and under-gunned. Within 72 hours, after the Germans had pushed forward more than 3 miles (5 km), it looked as if they might well take Verdun and its surrounding defenses. As Falkenhayn had predicted, however, the French were determined to hold out. Pouring men and munitions into the line, they resolved that the German forces would not pass.

What became known as the "hell of Verdun" raged on for the rest of the year. The French lost about 378,000 men but still were not quite bled to death. The Germans, on the other hand, lost almost as many themselves. Since they were also fighting on the Eastern Front, where they had to support Austria-Hungary, as well

Above: Happy to be out of the fight—German prisoners taken at Verdun are paraded through the streets under mounted guard on their way to captivity.

OVER THE TOP

British private soldier Roy Bealing remembers going over the top of his trench during an attack on the Somme:

"When the whistle went, I threw my rifle on top of the trench and clambered out of it, grabbed the rifle and started going forward. There were shell-holes everywhere. I hadn't gone far before I fell in one. . . . I must have fallen half a dozen times before I got to the first line, and there were lads falling all over the place. You didn't know whether they were just tripping up, like me, or whether they were going down with bullets in them, because it wasn't just the shells exploding round about, it was the machine guns hammering out like hell from the third German line because it was on slightly higher ground."

—Quoted in *Somme*, Lyn Macdonald

as supplying troops to other theaters of war, such as Africa and the Middle East, the losses were harder for them to bear. Also, in July, their assault on Verdun had drawn a massive British counterassault on the Somme.

THE SOMME

In late 1915 (*as we saw on page 29*), the Allies had planned a joint attack on the Somme for the late summer of 1916. This plan was altered when the Verdun offensive pinned down the bulk of the French Army. In response, the main weight of the Allied attack—which at the request of the French was brought forward by several weeks—would now be borne by the British.

Right: "Fix Bayonets!" British troops prepare to go over the top of their protective trench on the first day of the Battle of the Somme, July 1, 1916. For many, this was their first experience of battle; for most of the 60,000 killed and wounded, it was also their last.

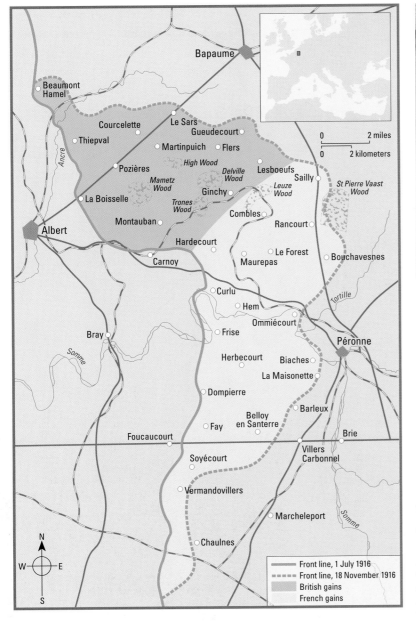

Above: Field Marshal Sir Douglas Haig (1861–1928), friend of British King George V and commander in chief of the British forces in France, 1915–18.

Left: The Battle of the Somme, 1916. The battleground was not chosen for strategic reasons, but because it was where the French and British lines met.

Before 1914, the British had concentrated their military spending on the Royal Navy. Their regular army ready for European action had consisted only of the 150,000-strong British Expeditionary Force. By 1916, this had been all but wiped out, meaning that the hugely expanded army—now over two million men— was largely made up of eager but inexperienced volunteers. They were joined by the small but highly efficient contingents provided by Canada, South Africa, New Zealand, and Australia. It was with these forces, domestic and colonial, that the new British commander, Sir Douglas Haig, hoped to break through the well arranged German defenses on the Somme.

The first day of the offensive— July 1, 1916—was the worst ever experienced by a British army. Despite careful preparation and a huge, eight-day preliminary bombardment of the enemy lines, the troops were forced to walk across "no man's land" into barbed wire and the deadly fire of machine guns—most of which had survived the artillery bombardment in deep concrete shelters. The attacking Allies were mowed down like grass. Some 58,000 men were lost for minimal gains. Only on the southern flank and in the neighboring French sector was much progress made.

The battle raged on until November, by which time the Allies had advanced no more than 10 miles (16 km) at a cost of 613,000 men killed and wounded (419,000 British). Even so, the German army had suffered equally heavy losses. Combined with the losses at Verdun and the Brusilov Offensive (*see below*), by the end of the year it was no longer fit to attack.

RUSSIA'S LAST ATTACK

As the British were attempting to take pressure off the French by attacking on the Somme, so the Russians had gathered themselves for one final offensive on the Eastern Front. They also planned to help their Italian allies by drawing Austro-Hungarian divisions away from the Alps. The general responsible for planning and launching the attack was Alexei Brusilov, probably the most capable Russian commander of the war.

Right: Russia's Brusilov Offensive in 1916 forced the Germans to switch troops from the Western Front but brought the Russian army to its knees.

Below: Tired of official incompetence and senseless slaughter, Russian soldiers surrender in 1917.

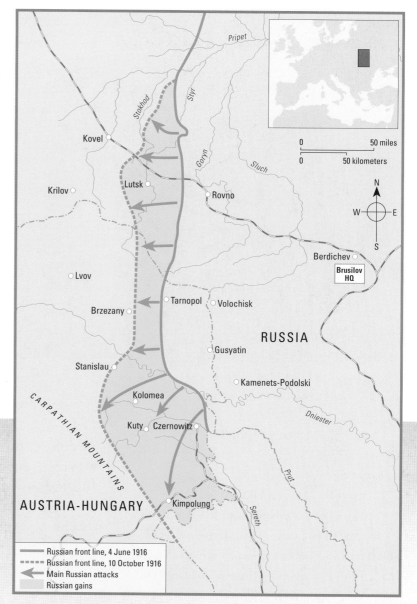

Russian front line, 4 June 1916
Russian front line, 10 October 1916
Main Russian attacks
Russian gains

The last czar of Russia, Nicholas II, sits alone after being forced to abdicate his throne in 1917.

What is now called the "Brusilov Offensive" began on June 4, 1916. The Russians moved forward in the valleys of the Prut Rivers and Dniester and further north toward the town of Lutsk. Brusilov placed himself between the two points of attack. His enemy, mostly Austro-Hungarian, was taken somewhat by surprise and fell back in disarray. Within two weeks, the Russians had advanced about 50 miles (80 km) and taken almost 100,000 prisoners.

Realizing the danger, both German and Austro-Hungarian reinforcements were rushed to the front and halted the Russian advance for a while. Twice that summer the Russians resumed their advance. They met with considerable success against the Austro-Hungarians in the south, where the Russians reached the Carpathian Mountains, but less against the Germans in the north. Finally, in mid-September, Brusilov called off his entire operation. His army had fought itself to a standstill, having lost about 1.4 million men as casualties and prisoners. The figure for his opponents was only slightly less.

Brusilov had been let down by his support services, not by his troops. Sometimes attacks were

THE RUSSIAN ARMY

The Russian 3rd, 7th, 8th, 9th, and 11th armies launched the Brusilov Offensive. Their strengths and varied make-up were as follows:

3rd Army
6 infantry divisions
6 cavalry divisions (5 of Cossacks)
1 reserve division

7th Army
9 infantry divisions
2 divisions of Finnish troops
2 cavalry divisions (1 of Cossacks)
3 reserve divisions, including 1 of Turks

8th Army
10 infantry divisions
2 divisions of Turkish troops
3 cavalry divisions (1 of Cossacks)
1 division of Finnish troops
2 reserve divisions

9th Army
9 infantry divisions
5 cavalry divisions (4 of Cossacks)
1 reserve division

11th Army
8 infantry divisions
4 cavalry divisions
1 division of Finnish troops
3 reserve divisions

Total initial strength of all armies:
57 infantry divisions (570,000 men approx.);
20 cavalry divisions (200,000 men approx.)

(Note: These numbers do not include troops who were brought in later)

halted because the ammunition ran out. On other occasions, reinforcements came too late because of the inefficiency of the Russian railway system. Supplies of food and new weapons were at best unreliable, and sometimes nonexistent. To top it all, the country's military leadership, from Supreme Commander Czar

Nicholas II on down, failed to cooperate with one another or coordinate their activities. In fact, after the Brusilov Offensive, the entire Russian military machine began to fall apart.

FRANCE GRINDS TO A HALT

The most interesting development on the Western Front during 1917 was that the Germans withdrew to the Hindenburg Line (*Siegfried Stellung*) that ran south in France from Arras to near Soissons. The Hindenburg Line was a preprepared defensive arrangement of barbed wire entanglements, trenches, machine gun posts, and concrete bunkers that proved exceptionally difficult to penetrate by conventional means. The Germans gave up any idea of launching an offensive in

Below: Germany's Hindenburg Line, 1916, peppered with many shell craters.

Above: An army falls apart—French deserters run toward the German lines, spring 1917. News of events such as this mutiny by serving soldiers was not revealed to the general public.

this part of the front and instead retired to these defended bunkers between February 23 and April 5. In contrast, the Allies still hoped for their elusive breakthrough. The new French commander, General Robert Nivelle, well known for his offensive strategies, believed he could break through the German lines in

the region of the River Aisne. His subordinates, including Marshal Philippe Pétain, strongly advised him to reconsider. He refused.

By way of a diversion, in April the British under Haig attacked near Arras. After the usual bombardment, they made the biggest single-day

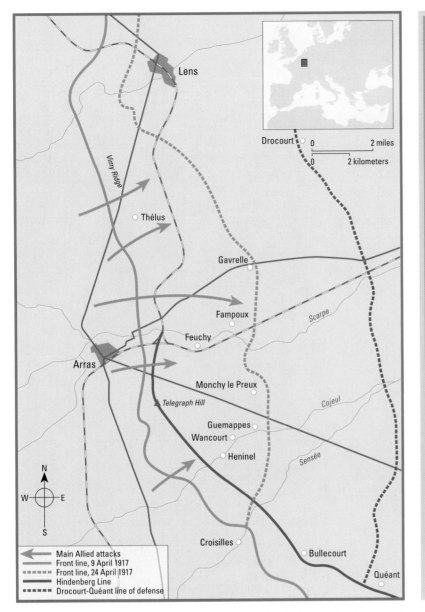

The Battle of Arras, 1917. Canadian forces seized Vimy Ridge in one of the most gallant actions of the entire war.

Map labels:
Lens
Drocourt
2 miles
2 kilometers
Vimy Ridge
Thélus
Gavrelle
Fampoux
Scarpe
Feuchy
Arras
Monchy le Preux
Telegraph Hill
Cojeul
Guemappes
Wancourt
Heninel
Sensée
Croisilles
Bullecourt
Quéant

N
W—E
S

Legend:
Main Allied attacks
Front line, 9 April 1917
Front line, 24 April 1917
Hindenberg Line
Drocourt-Quéant line of defense

GASSED

Harold Clegg recalls the effects of a German attack in July 1917 using a new form of gas—mustard gas—that burned away at the organs with which it came into contact:

"Our eyes now began to feel irritated. The tea was instrumental in making all and sundry commence to vomit. After being violently sick I received instructions to prepare myself to join a [guard] party . . . I began to scrape the . . . mud from my [equipment] . . .

"While doing so I heard several men complain about pain in their eyes, some even complaining of going blind."
–July 1917.

—Quoted in *The Imperial War Museum Book of the First World War*, edited by Malcolm Brown

advance of the war by British forces thus far—pathetically, less than 3.5 miles (5.5 km). Although the fighting continued to mid-May, further gains were very limited before the offensive was called off.

Meanwhile, the French had launched their offensive between Soissons and Reims (see *locations on page 29*). Yet again, despite the use of tanks (first seen on the Somme), a decisive breakthrough that could release the cavalry over open ground was not achieved. After some early gains, including the capture of 20,000 German soldiers and a section of the Hindenburg Line,

the advance floundered to a halt. The casualty rate had been as high as ever—in less than a month Nivelle lost 187,000 of the 1.2 million men under his command. The Germans' figure was about 163,000 losses.

The morale of many French troops now broke: a large number simply refused to take part in any further attacks. For a while (April to June 1917), the mutiny threatened to force France out of the war, making a German victory highly probable. Nivelle was promptly fired and, with great skill, Pétain began the difficult task of pulling his shattered forces together again.

Heavily laden British troops move up to the front line, October 1917, as the war of attrition goes on . . . and on.

THE GERMAN LINE HOLDS

1917 was the crucial year of the war. Russia was in turmoil (*see pages 40-41*). Austria-Hungary crushed the Italians (*see pages 18-19*), who were more and more disillusioned with the war. The bulk of the French were not able to do more than hold their line. The German command sensed that victory in the east was near and a sustained attack on the demoralized French line might, at last, achieve a breakthrough.

Field Marshal Douglas Haig, the British commander in chief, still believed he could pierce the German line with a massive frontal assault. On top of this came the dramatic development of April 6, 1917—the United States joined the war on the Allied side. Two factors in particular convinced Congress to take this momentous step. First, early in the year, Germany reintroduced unrestricted submarine warfare, which threatened the shipping of the neutral United States. Second, the British intercepted a German telegram offering part of the southern United States to Mexico if it would side with the Central Powers. When this information

THE ONLY ONE

Private R. Le Brun, a Canadian machine gunner, remembers fighting in the deep November mud around the village of Passchendaele:

"There was nothing between us and the Germans across the swamp. Three times during the night they shelled us heavily, and we had to keep on spraying bullets into the darkness to keep them from advancing. The night was alive with bullets. By morning, of our team of six, only my buddy Tombes and I were left. Then came the burst that got Tombes. It got him right in the head. . . . It was a terrible feeling being the only one left."

—Quoted in *They Called It Passchendaele*, Lyn Macdonald

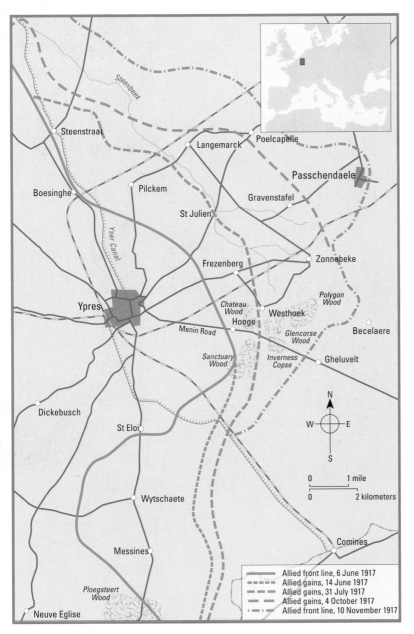

Left: The Third Battle of Ypres, 1917. British soldiers named it after the small, smashed village they eventually managed to capture—Passchendaele.

Above: U.S. President Woodrow Wilson led his country into the war in April 1917.

reached the U.S. government, war with Germany became inevitable.

Although U.S. naval forces made an immediate difference in the Atlantic, on land the U.S. intervention had no immediate impact. Its army was small and inefficient, and it was almost eighteen months before a large modern force could be raised, equipped, trained, and brought to bear on the enemy.

In the meantime, the British made one last effort to win the war on their own.

British Field Marshall Haig had spent eighteen months planning his July 1917 Ypres offensive. The Germans had spent almost as long preparing to meet it. The result was a titanic struggle similar to that which had taken place at Verdun the previous year. No breakthrough came, although

the British did manage to take the high ground that overlooked Ypres, including the village of Passchendaele. The 310,000 casualties that it cost, however, certainly hurt the British much as the French had been hurt the previous spring.

THE COLLAPSE OF
RUSSIA By unwisely assuming
overall command on the Eastern Front in September 1915, Czar Nicholas II of Russia sealed his own fate. From that time on, all

failures—and there were many—
would ultimately be laid his feet.
By the end of 1916, the country's
railway system had collapsed, and
millions of city dwellers faced
starvation as a result. The armed
forces were in chaos. The czar and
his government were thoroughly
discredited. Food riots, in March
1917, brought matters to a head.
The czar abdicated and was replaced
by a Western-style republican
government that promised to hold
free elections. It did not, however,
take Russia out of the war.

In July 1917, at the request of
his hard-pressed allies in the west,
Russian Prime Minister Alexander
Kerensky called for yet another
offensive. It lasted nineteen days.
The Central Powers launched
counterattacks. Along broad
stretches of the front, the Russian
soldiers simply threw down their
arms and fled. A further German
offensive in September pushed
closer to Petrograd (St. Petersburg).

Kerensky's unelected Provisional
Government staggered on until
November, when it was overthrown
in a communist coup in Petrograd.

The collapse of Russia on the Eastern Front, 1917–18. The German
advance brought vast industrial and agricultural wealth to Germany.

THE TREATY OF BREST-LITOVSK

Russia surrendered the following to the Central Powers:

Territory	Ukraine, Finland, Baltic Provinces (Estonia, Lithuania, Latvia), the Caucasus, Belorussia (White Russia), Poland.
Population	33 percent
Railway network	53 percent
Arable land	25 percent
Coal fields	70 percent
Total industry	40 percent

Trotsky hoped the communist revolution would spread from Russia to Germany and other countries, so he put off reaching an agreement with the Germans. They responded by advancing rapidly toward Petrograd. This forced Trotsky's hand. On March 3, 1918, Russia formally made peace, surrendering vast territories to the Germans, including the Ukraine, Finland, Poland, and much of its own industrial capacity. Germany was now free to concentrate all its resources on the Western Front in an attempt to win the war before U.S. power could turn the war in favor of the Allies.

Trotsky and Stalin, key members of the communist Bolshevik party, address crowds of supporters in Moscow, October 1917.

The communists, attracting support with their slogan, "Peace! Bread! Land!" rapidly extended their rule to Moscow and other cities. To provide the promised peace, the new leaders, Vladimir Lenin and Foreign Minister Leon Trotsky, signed an armistice with the Germans on December 3, 1917. Negotiations soon followed.

Right: Alexander Kerensky, Russia's liberal premier who alienated his countrymen by continuing the war with Germany. This allowed communists to gain popularity and power.

CHAPTER 4
VICTORY AND DEFEAT

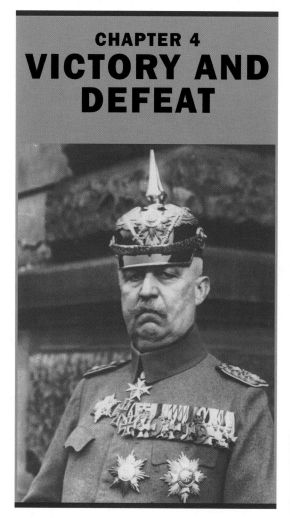

Above: General Erich von Ludendorff, who masterminded Germany's final offensive in the spring of 1918. He is pictured here after the war, in around 1924.

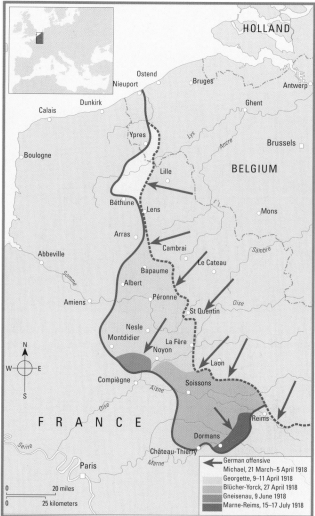

Map: Germany's spring offensives, 1918. A series of dramatic offensives in early 1918 recaptured in weeks territory that Germany had lost over the previous years.

German offensive
Michael, 21 March–5 April 1918
Georgette, 9–11 April 1918
Blücher-Yorck, 27 April 1918
Gneisenau, 9 June 1918
Marne-Reims, 15–17 July 1918

The final German offensives that would win or lose the war were masterminded by General Erich von Ludendorff. For this first attack, and the one about which he was most optimistic, he chose his ground carefully. His target was the lightly held British front on the old Somme battlefield, perhaps the weakest point in the enemy line. By mid-March 1918, he had transferred thousands of troops from the Eastern Front, assembling three German armies (sixty-three divisions or some 630,000 men) to face twenty-six divisions of the British Third and Fifth Armies.

The German assault began in thick fog on March 21. First came a 6,000-gun bombardment, many firing blistering mustard gas shells, then an advance all along the line. Overwhelmed, the British fell back. For a time, it looked as if the two British armies might be split apart, leaving the Germans free to sweep into the heart of France. To deal with the crisis, French Marshal Ferdinand Foch was appointed supreme commander of all Allied forces on the Western Front. Coordinating the resistance, he rushed French reinforcements to the front. Finally, having fallen back almost 50 miles (80 km) in places (the greatest movement of the trench war), the Allied line held fast. On April 5, Ludendorff called the operation off.

THE COST OF THE LUDENDORFF OFFENSIVES, MARCH–JUNE 1918

Casualties (killed and wounded)

	German	French	British	Total
Somme/Lys	348,000	112,000	343,000	803,000
Aisne	130,000	96,000	28,000	254,000
Oise	45,000	35,000		80,000
Total killed in four offensives				
	124,000	220,000	61,000	405,000

One of many thousands of British soldiers killed during the German offensives of 1918. This man died covering the retreat of his comrades.

Having failed to break through on the Somme, Ludendorff turned his attention to the line further north. Here he had located another weakly defended British sector, this time south of Ypres on the Lys River. Launching another gigantic attack, the Germans came extremely close to breaking through. Indeed, if Ludendorff had been less cautious in following up early progress, the Lys Offensive (April 9–29) might have led to a German victory.

Abandoning the Lys offensive, Ludendorff turned his attention to the French on the Aisne River (May 27–June 2) and in the Oise Valley (Noyon-Montdidier, June 9–13). As before, neither offensive made the anticipated progress. Despite suffering enormous casualties, the Allied line remained intact. Ludendorff's time was running out.

ALLIED ADVANCE

Ludendorff next planned a huge summer offensive for the Flanders

French Marshal Ferdinand Foch was given overall command of the Allies on the Western Front in 1918.

Blinded by an attack with poison gas during the Second Battle of the Marne (July 1918), two French soldiers are led to a field hospital by their comrades.

region, where the line was held by the British and Belgians. To tie down the French and prevent them from sending reinforcements north, on July 15, 1918, he launched an attack along the Marne River. Here, on the site of the first major battle of the war, three German armies advanced on either side of the famous Champagne city of Reims (*see page 29*).

A familiar pattern emerged. The Germans made some progress but were halted when the Allies managed to bring up reinforcements. On this occasion, however, the fighting did not stop there. To the Germans' surprise, on July 18, Foch ordered a counterattack. Backed by 350 tanks, the French drove the Germans back over the ground they had captured and beyond. Ludendorff urgently brought up reinforcements of his own and stopped the Allied advance by early August. Nevertheless, an attack had become a serious defeat, and plans for a further German offensive were canceled.

It was now the turn of the Allies to go on the offensive. Putting into effect Haig's plan, Foch's first goal was to eliminate the salients in the Allied line that

CROSSING THE OLD BATTLEFIELD

In the autumn of 1918, Major P. H. Pilditch cycled across the Somme battlefield searching for the grave of a friend killed in 1914:
"On the way back we spent some time in the old No Man's Land of four years' duration . . . It was a morbid but intensely interesting occupation tracing the various battles among the hundreds of skulls, bones and remains scattered thickly about. The progress of our successive attacks could be clearly seen from the types of equipment on the skeletons, soft caps denoting 1914 and early 1915, then respirators, then steel helmets marking attacks in 1916. . . . There were many of these poor remains all along the German wire."
—Quoted in *The Imperial War Museum Book of the First World War*, edited by Malcolm Brown

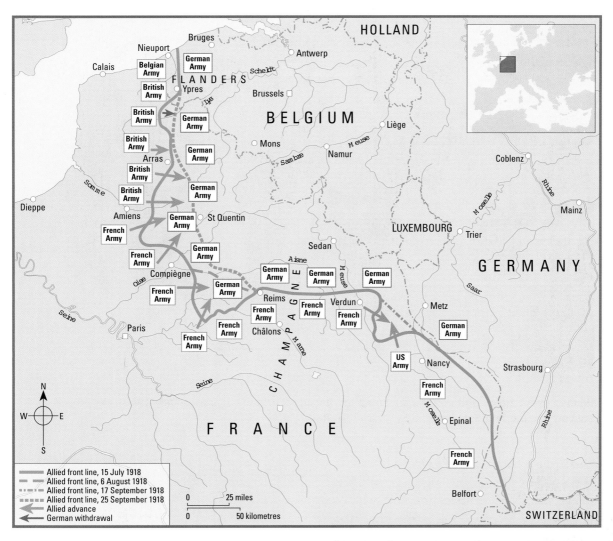

"Salient busting": the forceful term used to describe the Allied campaigns that pushed back the Germans and reduced the salients (bulges) in the front line on the Western Front, in July–September 1918.

had been created by the Ludendorff offensives. By August 5, 1918, the Aisne salient had been recovered. Then, on August 8, the Allies launched a large-scale attack to recapture the lost Somme battlefield east of Amiens. On a remarkable first day—the "black day of the German army"—British, French, and Canadian troops advanced almost 10 miles (16 km). They took six thousand prisoners and captured 100 guns. In some places the Germans, for the first time in the war, fled in disarray before the overwhelming onslaught of tanks, aircraft, artillery, and infantry.

Right: Some of the many thousands of German soldiers captured by the Allies during August 1918.

WORLD WAR I

The Allies pressed forward until early September, by which time the Germans had abandoned all the ground gained earlier and withdrawn to the Hindenburg Line. Thousands more prisoners had been taken and many more guns seized. As summer turned to autumn, the outlook for the German Army was looking bleaker by the day.

IMPACT OF THE UNITED STATES Having entered the war in April 1917, General John Pershing, the commander of the U.S. forces in France (the American Expeditionary Force, AEF) began to build a U.S. Army. By the end of the war, there were some two million U.S. troops in France, where they were trained and equipped. First to see action was the U.S. First Division, which on May 28, 1918, successfully

U.S. CASUALTIES ON THE WESTERN FRONT

Cantigny	1,600
Belleau Wood	8,800
Marne	40,000
St. Mihiel	7,000
Meuse-Argonne	117,000

Total in all theaters 281,000

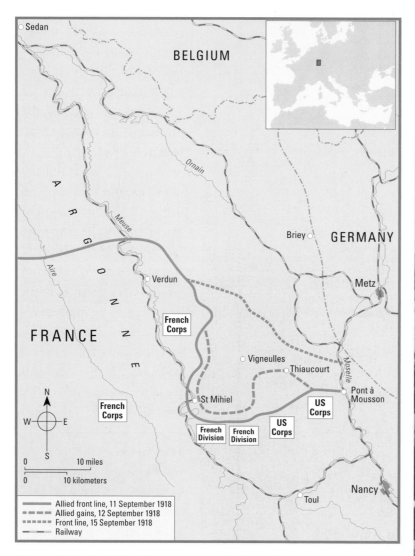

Above: Enter the United States—the St. Mihiel battlefield where U.S. forces made their first major contribution to the Allied victory.

Right: U.S. 18th Infantry Machine Gun Battalion troops move toward the front line near St. Mihiel, September 13, 1918.

captured the village of Cantigny during the German Aisne River offensive. A week later, the Second Division withstood a German attack and captured Belleau Wood near Château-Thierry. By the time of the Marne attack and counterattack (*see pages 44–45*), the U.S. had more than a quarter of a million men in the field. The U.S. First Army, however, was not fully ready for independent action until the end of the month.

The full impact of U.S. intervention was finally felt in September, during the Allied salient-busting operations. The U.S. First Army was given the task of reducing the St. Mihiel salient southeast of Verdun. Attacking on September 12, with 600 aircraft in support, the United States caught Germany in the process of withdrawing and cleared most of the salient in a single day. The message to their Allies and foe alike was obvious—the Americans were now a force to be reckoned with.

Above: The transatlantic alliance—U.S. General John Pershing (right), the commander of the American Expeditionary Force, with the Allied commander in chief, Marshal Foch of France.

From St. Mihiel, Pershing moved north of Verdun to work with the French in the massive Meuse-Argonne offensive that lasted to the end of the war (*see pages 48-49*). After good progress when the attack began, the Americans became bogged down in October and suffered heavy casualties. With more troops ready for battle each day, the AEF was now divided into two armies. By the time of the Armistice on November 11, 1918, they were once again making rapid progress and even beat the French in the "race to Sedan." As many had predicted in 1917, once the United States managed to mobilize its manpower, all hopes of a German victory disappeared.

CHAPTER 5
THE END OF THE WAR

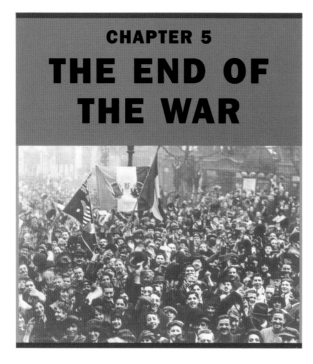

Armistice at last: Joyful Parisians celebrate the end of hostilities on the streets of the French capital on November 11, 1918.

Having removed the dangerous salients from their line, on September 26 the Allies began their final onslaught. Foch's master plan involved three offensives: a small Belgian attack forward of Ypres, larger forces of French and Americans in a pincer movement on the River Meuse swinging north of Verdun, and the British and French, in the largest attack, driving towards Cambrai and St. Quentin.

The southern Franco-American offensive was the first to begin. With overwhelming force, including air

The German High Seas Fleet surrenders to the British at Scapa Flow, Orkney, Scotland, on November 21, 1918.

superiority and large contingents of tanks, the Allies drove Germany steadily back, capturing Sedan on November 6. The armistice was signed as they got ready to move south over the German border to Metz. At the other end of the line the Belgians (with some support from other nations) advanced equally rapidly to Ostend and on toward Antwerp. To their south, the British, supported by French and U.S. divisions, took Cambrai, forced Germany to abandon the Hindenburg Line on October 4, and were pushing on towards Charleroi when hostilities ceased.

Hindenburg and Ludendorff had been virtually running Germany since early 1918. When their armies were pushed back so dramatically in the autumn, Ludendorff put out feelers for a ceasefire. The terms were unacceptable—Germany was asked to surrender all land occupied since 1870, dismantle its armed forces, surrender much of its martial equipment, and set aside its treaties with Russia and Romania.

As the war dragged on, Germany's allies began to desert. Bulgaria signed an armistice on September 29. Mounting starvation and discontent in Germany led to strikes and riots. When the German navy mutinied, revolution (as in Russia) became a real possibility. Accepting the inevitable, on October 26, Ludendorff resigned and fled to Sweden. Hindenburg remained at his post, but Turkey signed an armistice on October 30, as did Austria-Hungary on November 3. Finally, at 11 A.M. on November 11, Germany too accepted the Allies' terms, and the guns finally fell silent.

Below: The final Allied advance, autumn 1918. After the war, the Germans took pride in the fact that no foreign soldier had set foot on their soil.

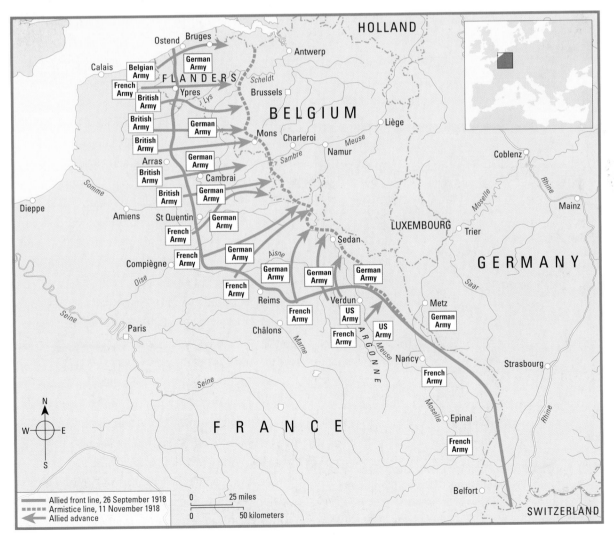

MAKING PEACE A series of long-negotiated treaties turned the various short-term armistices into what was hoped would be lasting peace. The Treaty of St. Germain organized the breakup of the Austro-Hungarian Empire, creating the separate states of Austria, Hungary, and Czechoslovakia (the Balkan peoples had already established themselves as Yugoslavia). As with the other treaties, it also limited the military capacity of the former Central Powers. At Neuilly (November 27, 1919) Bulgaria's frontiers were established. The terms of Hungary's surrender were sealed at Trianon on June 4, 1920. The Treaty of Trianon (August 10, 1920) broke up the Ottoman Empire, leaving the much smaller state of Turkey.

By far the most important treaty was that dealing with Germany. Signed at Versailles, France, on June 28, 1919, it was an extremely harsh document that the

> ## WHAT MIGHT HAVE BEEN . . .
>
> In introducing his Fourteen Points to the U.S. Congress on January 8, 1918, President Wilson spoke of the world he hoped would emerge after the war:
> *"What we demand in this war . . . is that the world be made fit and safe to live in; and particularly that it be made safe for every peace-loving nation which, like our own, wishes to live its own life, determine its own institutions, be assured of justice and fair dealings by the other peoples of the world, as against force and selfish aggression. All the peoples of the world are in effect partners in this interest . . . "*
> —Quoted in *Great Issues in American History: From Reconstruction to the Present Day, 1864-1969*, edited by Richard Hofstadter

Germans had no option but to accept. This was not what some peacemakers had envisioned in 1918. For example, in his Fourteen Points (January 1918), U.S. President Woodrow Wilson had set out a reasonable and moderate set of peace aims. At Versailles, these were overridden by the demands of French Prime Minister Georges Clemenceau and, to a lesser extent, British Prime Minister David Lloyd George. Both were driven by public opinion at home demanding vengeance after four and one-half years of slaughter.

With the Treaty of Versailles Germany lost all its colonies and some territory in Europe. It was obliged to accept total responsibility for the war, disband most of its armed forces, and pay the Allies an impossible 200 million gold marks (about 30 million dollars) in reparations (compensation) for war damage. Britain and France also took possession of the former Central Powers' colonies. As the popular cry ran, Germany had been squeezed "until the pips squeaked."

As many recognized at the time, the Versailles settlement was no recipe for long-term peace. It left the once proud Germany humiliated, weakened, and impoverished—ideal soil in which extremists might plant their wicked seeds of revenge. In this way, the ground was prepared for World War II, which broke out just over twenty years after the end of this "War to End All Wars."

(Left to right) Prime Minister David Lloyd George of Great Britain, Prime Minister Georges Clemenceau of France, and U.S. President Woodrow Wilson on their way to the Versailles peace talks, June 1919.

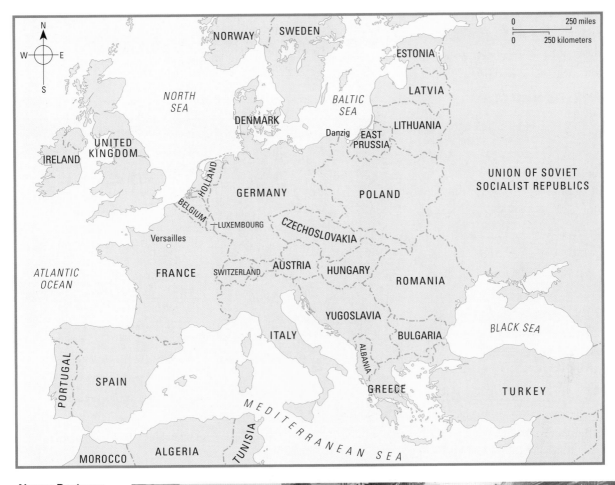

Above: Post-war Europe, showing the much-reduced Austria, Germany, Russia, and Turkey, and the host of new states, such as Czechoslovakia and Yugoslavia. Danzig was termed a Free City under League of Nations protection.

Right: Into the Roaring Twenties—thousands of delighted citizens turn out for a victory parade on New York's Fifth Avenue, 1919.

THE GENERALS

GENERAL ALEXEI BRUSILOV (1853–1926)

Unlike most World War I commanders, the energetic Alexei Brusilov showed both flair and imagination. Having made a name for himself in Russia's war with Turkey, 1877–78, he was key to Russia's advance into Galicia in 1914. His finest moment was the spectacular but ultimately unsuccessful offensive of 1916, which greatly helped his struggling French allies on the Western Front. After the war, he served with the communist Red Army.

MARSHAL FERDINAND FOCH (1851–1929)

Having lived under occupation in Lorraine, a province that France had surrendered to Germany after military defeat in 1871, Ferdinand Foch of France needed no motivation in his quest to drive out the invader. An author of two books on strategy, he distinguished himself at the Battle of the Marne (1914). For much of the war, he had called for all Allied forces to be under a single command. When the idea finally became reality in 1918, the task fell to him. Showing great skill, insight, and tact, he

masterminded the successful Allied offensives of the final months of the war.

FIELD MARSHAL DOUGLAS HAIG (1861–1928)

Douglas Haig is one of the most controversial military commanders in British history. His supporters refer to his steely character, his determination to succeed against all odds (a man of powerful faith, he seemed to have believed that God was guiding him), and his skillful offensives of 1918. Opponents accuse him of being rigid in strategy and insensitive to human losses, particularly during the British Somme, Arras, and Passchendaele offensives, 1916–17.

FIELD MARSHAL PAUL VON HINDENBURG (1847–1934)

The aristocratic Paul von Hindenburg went to army cadet school at the age of eleven and then went on to serve with distinction until retirement in 1911. On the outbreak of war, he was recalled to service and sent, with the more able second-in-command Ludendorff, to meet the Russian attack on Prussia. His reputation was made by victories at Tannenberg and Masurian Lakes. Placed in overall command of Central Powers strategy in 1916, he concentrated, unsuccessfully, on defense. He was elected president of Germany in 1925, and, in a choice that soon changed history, appointed Adolf Hitler to be German chancellor in 1933.

GENERAL FRANZ CONRAD VON HOTZENDORF (1852–1925)

Having been put in charge of the Austrian Army in 1906, Franz Conrad was eager for war with Serbia and Italy. When war came, however, he found it more challenging than he expected, especially against Serbia. In the end, his most likely chance of success—against Italy in 1916—was cut short by the Brusilov Offensive. He was put under Hindenburg's overall command in September 1916 and was dismissed the following year.

MUSTAFA KEMAL (1881–1938)

Known in later life as the "father of the Turks" (*Ataturk*), Kemal played a vital role in resisting the Allied landings in Gallipoli in 1916. He then fought with distinction in the Caucasus, remaining the only undefeated Turkish commander. As the first president of the new Turkish Republic (1924), he crowned his military career with an even more successful one as a modernizing politician.

GENERAL ERICH VON LUDENDORFF (1865–1937)

Extremely able but occasionally flawed in judgment, von Ludendorff helped rearrange the Schlieffen Plan (*see pages 6–7*) and guided Hindenburg in the key victories against Russia in 1914. Thereafter, Hindenburg and Ludendorff worked closely together, becoming virtual masters of Germany by 1918. Having almost won the war with his 1918 spring offensives, Ludendorff's fortunes declined rapidly. He fled to Sweden in disguise in 1918, reemerging after the war as a Nazi politician.

GENERAL HELMUTH VON MOLTKE (1848–1916)

Nephew of one of Prussia's greatest generals, Helmuth von Moltke (sometimes known as "von Moltke the Younger") is mainly remembered for working with Ludendorff to alter the Schlieffen Plan to attack western France. By weakening the German right flank, which was to sweep down to the west of Paris, he was partly responsible for the failure of the German strategy at the Battle of the Marne, 1914. He was dismissed two days later.

GENERAL JOHN JOSEPH PERSHING (1860–1948)

John Pershing's U.S. military experience, gained in small scale encounters such as chasing bandits in Mexico, hardly prepared him for what he was to meet on the Western Front. Appointed to command of the American Expeditionary Force (AEF) in 1917, however, he built it up into an effective fighting force. Although Clemenceau called for his dismissal after a poor showing in the Argonne Forest, the idea was rejected and Pershing's armies played an important part in the Allies' last offensives of 1918.

MARSHAL PHILIPPE PÉTAIN (1856–1951)

Philippe Pétain, an avid student of war, realized earlier than most experts that offensives against artillery, barbed wire, and machine guns would be virtually impossible. His advice was ignored. Not until the Germans threatened breakthrough at Verdun in February 1917 did he get the chance to put his ideas to the test. His dramatic defense of Verdun made him a national hero, and he was made commander in chief of the French Army in May 1917. Tragically, the "hero of Verdun" ended his life in prison for treacherous cooperation with the Nazis in World War II.

THE POLITICIANS

GEORGES CLEMENCEAU (1841–1929)

French Prime Minister. A tough and energetic man of peasant stock, the seventy-six-year-old Clemenceau (nicknamed "the Tiger") took over the leadership of France in the grim days of 1917. His speeches and his single-minded dedication to win the war and preserve France lifted the nation's morale and guided it to victory the following year. A strong admirer of the United States, he was always eager for it to join the Allies.

DAVID LLOYD GEORGE (1863–1945)

British Prime Minister Lloyd George had doubts about going to war but changed his mind after the German invasion of Belgium. Thereafter, as Minister of Munitions and Prime Minister (December 1916 onward), he used his considerable skills to gear the nation's industrial might to winning the war. As a radical, he did not always see eye to eye with high-born military commanders.

NICHOLAS II (1868–1918)

Czar of Russia. Russia could hardly have had a less suitable leader during World War I. Nicholas, the hereditary czar, was not blessed with intelligence or insight. He chose poor ministers and generals and allowed his court to become a nest of scandal. He abdicated in 1917 and was executed with his family by the communists in 1918.

WILHELM II (1859–1941)

Emperor of Germany. Lacking skill in the world of international politics, Wilhelm II (emperor or kaiser from 1888) occasionally upset relations with Britain through tactless statements and actions. His offer to support Austria-Hungary against Serbia in 1914 made war likely, and his influence then declined. He abdicated on November 9, 1918, and fled the country.

WOODROW WILSON (1856–1924)

In some ways the most statesmanlike of the war leaders, the idealistic Wilson worked as an academic before being elected U.S. president in 1912. He reluctantly took his country to war in 1917, then worked tirelessly for a better world once victory had been achieved. Sadly, having moderated his allies' calls for vengeance at Versailles, illness prevented him from taking his plans further.

STATISTICS CONCERNING COMBATANT NATIONS

All statistics taken from John Ellis and Michael Cox, eds., *The World War I Databook*, Aurum Press, 1993.

AGGREGATE MILITARY CASUALTIES AND CIVILIAN DEATHS 1914–18

Country	Population (millions)	Number Served in Forces (millions)	Force Casualties Killed and Missing	Wounded	P.O.W.	Total Killed, Wounded & Missing	Total Civilian Deaths
Australia	4.87	0.42	53,560	155,130	3,650	208,690	–
Austria-Hungary	49.90	7.80	539,630	1,943,240	2,118,190	2,482,870	?
Belgium	7.52	0.27	38,170	44,690	10,200	82,860	30,000
Bulgaria	5.50	1.20	77,450	152,400	10,620	229,850	275,000
Canada	7.40	0.62	58,990	149,710	2,820	208,700	–
France	39.60	8.66	1,385,300	4,329,200	446,300	5,714,500	40,000
Germany	67.00	13.40	2,037,000	5,687,000	993,800	7,724,000	700,000
Greece	4.80	0.28	5,000	20,000	c.1,000	25,000	130,000
India	316.00	1.68	62,060	66,690	11,070	128,750	–
Italy	35.00	5.90	462,400	955,000	530,000	1,417,400	?
Japan	67.20	0.80	?	?	–	1,970	–
New Zealand	1.05	0.13	16,710	41,320	500	58,030	–
Portugal	6.00	0.20	7,220	13,751	6,680	20,971	–
Romania	7.51	?	219,800	120,000	c.60,000	339,800	265,000 to 500,000
Russia	167.00	12.00	1,800,000	4,950,000	3,910,000	6,750,000	2,000,000
Serbia	5.00	0.71	127,500	133,150	70,000	260,650	600,000
South Africa	6.00	0.23	7,120	12,030	1,540	19,150	?
Turkey	21.30	0.99	236,000	770,000	145,000	1,006,000	2,000,000
United Kingdom	46.40	5.70	702,410	1,662,625	170,389	2,365,035	1,386
United States	92.00	4.35	51,822	230,074	4,434	281,896	–

AGGREGATE NAVAL LOSSES OF THE MAJOR POWERS, BY TYPE OF SHIP, AND AGGREGATE PERSONNEL LOSSES 1914–18

	UK	France	Russia	Italy	Japan	U.S.	Total	Germany	Aus.-Hungary	Turkey	Total
Battleship	13	4	2	3	1	–	23	1	3	2	6
Battlecruiser	3	–	–	–	1	–	4	1	–	–	1
Cruiser	13	5	2	3	–	1	24	6	2	1	9
Light Cruiser	12	–	1	–	2	–	15	18	–	–	18
Monitor	5	–	–	2	–	–	7	–	3	–	3
Torpedo Gunboat	5	3	–	–	–	–	8	–	–	–	–
Sloop	18	–	3	–	–	–	21	–	–	9	9
Destroyer	67	15	6	8	1	2	99	}109	6	1	}126
Torpedo Boat	11	10	9	4	1	–	35		8	2	
Aircraft Carrier	3	–	–	–	–	–	3	–	–	–	–
Minelayer	2	2	5	–	–	–	9	–	–	1	1
Minesweeper	–	–	30	2	–	1	33	29	–	2	31

UK	France	Russia	Italy	Japan	U.S.	Total	Germany	A-Hungary	Turkey	Total
Submarine	54	14	12	11	–	91	178	7	–	185
Personnel:										
killed	34,650	} 15,650	?	3,170	} 8,106	?	} 78,300	980	?	?
wounded	4,510		?	5,250		?		310	?	?

ANNUAL GERMAN U-BOAT LOSSES BY LOCALITY 1914–18

	North Sea, Orkneys and Shetlands	English Channel and Belgian Coast	North Channel, Irish Sea, Bristol Channel	North Atlantic	South Atlantic (south of Scilly Isles)	Baltic	Mediter-ranean	Black Sea and Bosphorous	Unknown	Total
1914	3	2	–	–	–	–	–	–	–	5
1915	10	2	1	1	2	1	–	1	1	19
1916	8	2	1	4	–	1	1	3	2	22
1917	13	13	4	25	5	1	2	–	–	63
1918	13	9	9	14	10	–	12	–	2	69
Total	47	28	15	44	17	3	15	4	5	178

BRITISH, OTHER ALLIED, AND NEUTRAL MERCHANT SHIPPING LOST THROUGH ENEMY ACTION 1914–18 (GROSS TONNAGE*)

	British	Allied and Neutral	Total
1914 August	44,692	18,075	62,767
1914 September	89,251	9,127	98,378
1914 October	78,088	9,829	87,917
1914 November	9,348	10,065	19,413
1914 December	26,815	17,382	44,197
TOTAL	**248,194**	**64,478**	**312,672**
1915 January	32,276	15,705	47,981
1915 February	36,372	23,549	59,921
1915 March	71,768	9,007	80,775
1915 April	24,383	31,342	55,725
1915 May	89,673	30,385	120,058
1915 June	91,315	40,113	131,428
1915 July	57,274	52,366	109,640
1915 August	151,354	34,512	185,866
1915 September	102,135	49,749	151,884
1915 October	54,156	34,378	88,534
1915 November	94,655	58,388	153,043
1915 December	74,490	48,651	123,141
TOTAL	**879,851**	**428,145**	**1,307,996**
1916 January	62,645	18,614	81,259
1916 February	75,928	41,619	117,547
1916 March	99,696	67,401	167,097
1916 April	141,409	50,258	191,667
1916 May	64,722	64,453	129,175
1916 June	36,976	71,879	108,855
1916 July	85,228	32,987	118,215
1916 August	45,026	117,718	162,744
1916 September	109,263	121,197	230,460
1916 October	177,386	176,274	353,660
1916 November	170,409	141,099	311,508
1916 December	182,728	172,411	355,139
TOTAL	**1,251,416**	**1,075,910**	**2,327,326**
1917 January	155,686	212,835	368,521
1917 February	316,964	223,042	540,006
1917 March	357,064	236,777	593,841
1917 April	551,202	329,825	881,027
1917 May	353,737	242,892	596,629
1917 June	419,267	268,240	687,507
1917 July	367,594	190,394	557,988
1917 August	330,052	181,678	511,730
1917 September	196,457	155,291	351,748
1917 October	276,359	182,199	458,558
1917 November	173,647	115,565	289,212
1917 December	253,500	145,611	399,111
TOTAL	**3,751,529**	**2,484,349**	**6,235,878**
1918 January	180,348	126,310	306,658
1918 February	227,582	91,375	318,957
1918 March	199,751	142,846	342,597
1918 April	215,784	62,935	278,719
1918 May	192,938	102,582	295,520
1918 June	163,629	91,958	255,587
1918 July	166,004	130,963	296,967
1918 August	147,257	136,558	283,815
1918 September	137,001	50,880	187,881
1918 October	59,229	59,330	118,559
1918 November	10,220	7,462	17,682
TOTAL	**1,699,743**	**1,003,199**	**2,666,942**
GRAND TOTAL	**7,830,733**	**5,056,081**	**12,886,814**

*recorded in metric tonnes

1830
Greece gains independence from the Turkish Empire.

1839
Treaty of London guarantees the neutrality of Belgium.

1859–70
Kingdom of Italy created.

1861
Romania formed.

1870–71
Franco-Prussian War.

JANUARY 1871
German Empire proclaimed at Versailles.

MAY 1871
Treaty of Paris. France cedes Alsace and Lorraine to Germany.

1878
Congress of Berlin. Serbia, Bosnia-Herzegovina, Bulgaria, Montenegro, and Romania granted independence from Turkey.

1879
Austro-German Dual Alliance.

1882
Italy agrees to Triple Alliance with Germany and Austria-Hungary.

1888
Wilhelm II becomes Kaiser (emperor) of Germany.

1894
Franco-Russian Alliance signed.

1898
Germany begins its naval build-up.

1902
Anglo-Japanese Alliance.

1904
Anglo-French *entente cordiale*.

1905
Schlieffen Plan drawn up.

1907
British Expeditionary Force formed.
Anglo-Russian entente.

1908
Austria-Hungary annexes Bosnia and Herzegovina.

1912
Woodrow Wilson elected president of the United States.

1912–13
Two Balkan Wars.

JANUARY 1914
German officer commands Constantinople garrison in Turkey.

JUNE 28, 1914
Austrian Archduke Franz Ferdinand assassinated in Sarajevo, Bosnia.

JULY 28, 1914
Austria-Hungary declares war on Serbia. Russia mobilizes.

AUGUST 1, 1914
Germany declares war on Russia. France mobilizes.

AUGUST 3, 1914
Germany declares war on France.

AUGUST 4, 1914
German troops enter Belgium. (Midnight) Britain declares war on Germany.

AUGUST 12, 1914
Britain and France declare war on Austria-Hungary.

23 AUGUST 1914
Japan joins Allies.

AUGUST 26–30, 1914
Germans defeat Russians at Tannenberg (*see photo, above*).

SEPTEMBER 5–9, 1914
German advance on the Western Front stopped at the Battle of the Marne.

SEPTEMBER 9–14, 1914
Germans defeat Russians at Masurian Lakes.

SEPTEMBER 14, 1914
Falkenhayn becomes German commander in chief.

OCTOBER 29, 1914
Turkey joins Central Powers.

OCTOBER 30–NOVEMBER 4, 1914
First Battle of Ypres.

NOVEMBER 1914
Russian advances in Galicia.

DECEMBER 29 1914–JANUARY 3, 1915
Russians defeat Turks at Sarikamish.

FEBRUARY 1915
Germany begins unrestricted submarine warfare (to September). Allied naval forces fail to pass through the Dardanelles.

MARCH 1915
Allied offensive at Neuve-Chapelle.

APRIL 25, 1915
Allies land at Gallipoli.

APRIL–MAY 1915
Second Battle of Ypres—first use of poison gas.

MAY 1915
Italy joins Allies.
Allied offensive in Artois. Germans making gains on Eastern Front.

AUGUST 1915
Germans capture Warsaw (Poland). Nicholas II takes command of Russian armies.

SEPTEMBER 1915
French offensive in Champagne. Allied Artois-Loos offensive (to November). Bulgaria joins Central Powers. Serbia overwhelmed.

OCTOBER 1915
Allies land at Salonika in Greece.

DECEMBER 1915
Joffre becomes French commander in chief. Haig becomes British commander in chief.

21 FEBRUARY 1916
German attack on Verdun, France, begins (to December). Pétain ordered to defend Verdun.

31 MAY-1 JUNE 1916
Battle of Jutland (*see photo, below*).

JUNE 4, 1916
Brusilov offensive begins (to September).

JULY 1, 1916
British Somme offensive begins (to November) (*see photo, right*).

AUGUST 1916
Romania joins Allies. Hindenburg replaces Falkenhayn as German commander in chief.

DECEMBER 1916
Lloyd George becomes British prime minister. Nivelle becomes French commander in chief.

JANUARY 1917
Zimmerman telegram urging Mexico to attack United States in alliance with Germany intercepted.

FEBRUARY 1917
Germans begin to fall back to Hindenburg Line. Germany reintroduces unrestricted submarine warfare.

MARCH 1917
Nicholas II abdicates after revolution in Russia. British take Baghdad in Mesopotamia.

APRIL 6, 1917
United States declares war on Germany.

APRIL 9–MAY 16, 1917
British offensive at Arras.
APRIL 16–MAY 9, 1917

Nivelle's disastrous offensive on River Aisne.

MAY 1917
Allies introduce convoys to protect merchant shipping. Pétain becomes French commander in chief.

JUNE 1917
First U.S. troops land in France.

JULY 1917
Russia's Kerensky offensive on Eastern Front.

JULY 31, 1917
Third Battle of Ypres (Passchendaele) begins (to November).

SEPTEMBER 1917
Germans advance on Petrograd, Russia.

OCTOBER 24–NOVEMBER 12, 1917
Italians defeated at Caporetto, Italy.

NOVEMBER 1917
Communist revolution in Russia. Clemenceau becomes prime minister of France.

DECEMBER 1917
British take Jerusalem.

1918
Civil War in Russia (to 1921).

JANUARY 1918
Wilson puts forward his Fourteen Points.

MARCH 3, 1918
Germany and Russia sign Treaty of Brest-Litovsk (*see photo, right*).

MARCH 21–APRIL 5, 1918
Ludendorff offensive on Somme. Foch appointed to be supreme commander of Allied forces.

APRIL 9–29, 1918
Ludendorff's Lys offensive.

MAY 27–JUNE 2, 1918
Ludendorff's offensive on Aisne River.

MAY 28, 1918
U.S. forces see action at Cantigny.

JUNE 9–13, 1918
Ludendorff's offensive on the Oise River.

JULY 15–AUGUST 5, 1918
Ludendorff's last offensive, on the Marne, met by Foch's counterattack.

AUGUST 8–SEPTEMBER 4, 1918
Allied Amiens offensive.

SEPTEMBER 12–16, 1918
U.S. offensive at St. Mihiel.

SEPTEMBER 26, 1918
Allies launch Meuse-Argonne offensive (*see photo, below*).

SEPTEMBER 27, 1918
Allies launch Cambrai-St. Quentin and Flanders offensives.

SEPTEMBER 29, 1918
Bulgaria signs an armistice.

OCTOBER 1, 1918
British take Damascus in Syria.

OCTOBER 4, 1918
Germans abandon Hindenburg Line.

OCTOBER 23–NOVEMBER 1918
Austro-Hungarians overwhelmed on Italian Front.

OCTOBER 30, 1918
Turkey signs armistice.

NOVEMBER 3, 1918
Austria-Hungary signs armistice.

NOVEMBER 6, 1918
Allies take Sedan.

NOVEMBER 11, 1918
Armistice on Western Front.

JANUARY 1919
Paris Peace Conference opens at Versailles.

JUNE 28, 1919
Germany signs Treaty of Versailles.

SEPTEMBER 10, 1919
Austria signs Treaty of St. Germain en Laye.

NOVEMBER 27, 1919
Bulgaria signs Treaty of Neuilly.

JUNE 4, 1920
Hungary signs Treaty of Trianon.

AUGUST 10, 1920
Turkey signs Treaty of Sèvres.

GLOSSARY

abdicate To step down as a monarch as a deliberate choice.

AEF American Expeditionary Force, the U.S. troops in Europe.

alliance An agreement between countries for their mutual help in time of war.

Allies, the Russia, France, Britain, Belgium, Italy, the United States, and the countries that fought in support with them in World War I.

ally A country that has formally agreed to assist another, usually in war.

annex To take over; to add or attach territory.

ANZAC Australia and New Zealand Army Corps.

armistice Cease-fire.

arms race Two or more countries trying to outdo each other by building up their armed forces.

artillery Heavy guns.

assassinate To murder a well-known figure, usually for political reasons.

attrition The wearing down of the enemy.

Austria-Hungary Empire of Austria and Hungary, joined in 1867.

autocratic All-powerful.

BEF British Expeditionary Force, British troops on the Western Front.

Balkans Region between the Black Sea and the Adriatic.

blockade Cutting off supplies.

blockhouse Concrete shelter.

brigade Army unit of about 1,000 men.

bombardment Continuous heavy artillery attack.

bureaucracy Civil service.

cabinet Leading members of a government.

capital Main city in a country, where government is located.

casualty Soldier killed or wounded.

cavalry Soldiers who fight on horseback.

Central Powers Germany, Austria-Hungary, Turkey, and Bulgaria.

colony Territory, usually overseas, seized by an empire.

communism System of government which outlaws private ownership of property and seeks to make sure that wealth is distributed equally among all people.

conference A high-level meeting.

Congress U.S. formal legislative assembly, consisting of the democratically elected Senate and the House of Representatives.

contingent Group of soldiers.

convoy Many merchant ships travelling together under the escort of warships.

Cossacks Tribal cavalrymen from southern Russia.

coup Sudden attempt to seize power.

Czar Russian emperor.

Dardanelles The narrow strip of water between the Bosphorus and the Aegean.

deadlock When neither side in a conflict is able to make progress.

depleted Run down.

depth charge Explosive device timed to go off at a preset depth to damage a submarine.

disband To break up an armed force.

division Army unit of about 10,000 men.

dog-fight One-to-one combat between fighter aircraft.

dreadnought A fast, heavily armored battleship.

Eastern Front Battle front between the Central Powers and Russia.

empire Many territories, often in different parts of the world, ruled by the same government.

engagement Military battle or encounter.

entente Informal agreement.

fiasco Farcical disaster.

flank The side of a military formation.

front The place where two opposing forces meet.

franco Referring to France or the French.

garrison Troops in a regular base.

Grand Fleet Britain's main battle fleet in World War I.

guerrillas Irregular soldiers who avoid set-piece conflicts and tend to fight free-style.

High Seas Fleet Germany's main battle fleet in World War I.

Hindenburg Line German preprepared defensive line on the Western Front.

home front Civilian support away from the battle front.

imperial Belonging to an empire.

infantry Foot soldiers.

mine Naval bomb, either floating on or under the surface of the sea.

minister Person responsible for an area of government, such as war or finance.

monitor To keep an eye on or keep track of.

morale The mood or spirit of a people at war.

munitions Provisions of war, such as bullets and guns.

mutiny To refuse to obey orders or fight.

neutral Not taking sides in a conflict.

no-man's-land The narrow strip of land between two front lines.

obsolete Out of date.

offensive A large-scale attack.

outflank To go around the side of.

peninsula Area of land surrounded on three sides by water.

prime minister Leading or chief minister, the head of government.

province Part of a country or empire.

Prussia Area of eastern Germany around Berlin.

radical Wanting profound change.

reconnaissance Searching for information about the landscape and any enemy forces on it.

reinforcements Extra troops.

reparations Compensation payments.

revolution A complete, swift, and permanent change in government.

salient Bulge in the front line that extends into enemy territory.

salient-busting Eliminating bulges (salients) in the enemy's front line.

Schlieffen Plan German war plan, drawn up in 1905 and later modified, to defeat France before Russia.

sector Part or section.

shell A projectile fired from a gun, containing an explosive charge and/or shrapnel balls propelled by a charge, which can either be contained in the shell case or loaded into the gun separately.

spotter aircraft Reconnaissance plane.

stalemate Position where no side appears to be able to win; deadlock.

strategy Overall war plans.

theater of war Area where fighting takes place.

torpedo Self-propelled underwater missile.

turbine Engine driven by fan blades.

turret Swivelling armored gun emplacement on a ship.

U-boat German submarine.

undermanned Without sufficient people to carry out a plan.

unrestricted Unlimited.

Western Front Front lines between the Allies and the Central Powers in France and Belgium.

Zeppelin German military airship.

FURTHER INFORMATION

RECOMMENDED BOOKS

Adams, Simon. *World War I*. DK Publishing, Inc., 2001.

Conway, Jophn R. *World War I: A Myreportlinks.COM Book*. Enslow Publishers, Inc., 2003.

Grant, Reg. *Armistice, 1918*. Raintree Publishers, 2001.

Levine, Beth Seidel. *When Christmas Comes Again: The World War I Diary of Simone Spencer*. Scholastic, Inc., 2002.

MacMillan, Margaret. *Paris, 1919: Six Months That Changed the World*. Random House, 2003.

Mair, Craig. *Britain at War, 1914–1919*. John Murray, 1989.

Massie, Robert K. *Castles of Steel*. Random House, 2003.

Ross, Stewart. *Battle of the Somme*. Raintree Publishers, 2004.

Ross, Stewart. *Causes of the First World War*. Raintree Publishers, 1998.

Wrenn, Andrew. *The First World War*. Cambridge University Press, 1998.

RECOMMENDED VIDEOS

The Great War, part of the multi-volume *United States History Origins to 2000* DVD series, 2003.

The Russian Revolution, 1995.

The Shot That Started the Great War, 1997.

World War I: Cause and Effect, 1999.

1910s: The Modern Age Begins, 2000.

World War I and the Interwar Years–Vol. 1, part of the *Archives of War* series, 1998.

World Wars and the Quest for Order: The Early 20th Century, History Through Literature series, 1998.

World War I Years (1917-1920), 2003.

RECOMMENDED WEBSITES

www.chs.k12.nf.ca/web2003/grassroots/causes_0 3/CAUSES2.htm.

Explore this site to delve more deeply into causes and conditions that led up toWorld War I.

www.schoolshistory.org.uk/firstworldwar.htm

Discover technological advances, interactional activities, other World War I links, teacher resources, and more.

www.worldwar1.com/bioindex.htm

Find a variety of biograpies and photographs of World War I figures.

www.spartacus.schoolnet.co.uk/FWWpolitical.htm

Obtain online history lessons, supplementary background material, and downloadable teacher resources.

www.worldwar1.com/

A History.com affiliate, World War I Trenches on the Web provides information on people, places, and events of the time, as well as a gallery of pictures of the war, with multiple translation services.

wpafb.af.mil/museum/history/ww1/ww1.htm

Download a video clip on World War I and tour the museum's gallery, among other things.

Note to parents and teachers

Every effort has been made by the publishers to ensure that these web sites are suitable for children; that they are of the highest educational value; and that they contain no inappropriate or offensive material. The nature of the Internet makes it impossible to guarantee that the contents of these sites will not be altered. We strongly advise that a responsible adult supervises Internet access.

PLACES TO VISIT

Imperial War Museum, London.
www.iwm.org.uk/lambeth/

National Army Museum, London.
www.national-army-museum.ac.uk/

Smithsonian National Air and Space Museum, Flagship Building on the National Mall, Washington D.C.
www.nasm.si.edu/exhibitions/gal206/gal206.html

Smithsonian Steven F. Udvar-Hazy Center, 14390 Air and Space Museum Parkway, Chantilly, VA.
www.nasm.si.edu/exhibitions/gal206/gal206.html

USAF Museum, Wright-Patterson Air Force Base, Dayton, Ohio.
www.wpafb.af.mil/museum/usafm.htm

ABOUT THE AUTHOR

The author, Stewart Ross, spent several years teaching at a variety of institutions in Britain, the United States, and Asia, before becoming a full-time writer in 1991. Since then he has published numerous books for children and adults, including *Leaders of World War I* and *The Technology of World War I*.

INDEX